UNMASKING
The Satanic Attack Against
MASCULINITY

TO:
Sister Lonnie Davis
Be Blessed
Wesley T. Leonard

UNMASKING
The Satanic Attack Against
MASCULINITY
What Both Women and Men Need to Know

MINISTER WESLEY T. LEONARD
& DR. CLEAVON P. MATTHEWS SR.

XULON PRESS

Xulon Press
2301 Lucien Way #415
Maitland, FL 32751
407.339.4217
www.xulonpress.com

ISBN-13: 9781545604939

DEDICATION

For my father John W. Leonard, in memoriam, who shaped me into the man I am today.

Dedicated to my son Johnathan Wesley Leonard, whom I've helped shape into the man he is today, and to my grandson Cailen Wesley Skinner, with prayer and supplication that I'm shaping into the man he should become. I also dedicate this book to other men in prayer with the hopes of providing valuable information to shape them into the men they should be.   *~Wesley T. Leonard*

To my beloved Father James E. Matthews, my Sons Cleavon Jr, Edward, Nephew Isaiah, and Grandson   *Gabriel Cleavon Sr*

PREFACE

There has been a tremendous shift in the perception of masculinity over the last few decades. Biblical masculinity is mocked on television, major news networks, and social media. There is an attack on the unique qualities of men. Advertisements featuring influential people celebrate the emasculation of men and denigrate their personalities.

This work is a response to this attack against biblical masculinity. It is not intended to condemn any individual or group of individuals who choose to embrace lifestyles that differ from biblical principles. Neither is it an attempt to minimize the importance and value of women who often serve as the backbone of many families. We believe in the dignity of every human being and that God has given each of us free will to choose our lives' paths.

Our objective is to create a dialogue that also values those of us choosing to live by a biblical masculinity which honors God and loves family, church, and society. We do not want men to become lost in the enemy's scheme to eliminate the value and importance of those willing to stand for the truth of God.

Each chapter will end with discussion questions that are ideal for small group studies for men, women, youth, or church bible studies. This is our call for the people of God to stand against the wiles of the Devil and clothe ourselves in the full armor of the Lord (Eph. 6).

Chapter 1

THE SATANIC ATTACK AGAINST MOSES

The Bible outlines the excuses we men use to perpetuate Satan's attack against us. Note Moses' excuses and self-deprecating reasons as to why he could not lead God's people even though he had been sent with God's blessing. Moses in the following list used Satan's attack to tell God in every way he could that he was not worthy of the task.

According to Moses, he was not good enough (Exodus 3:11). Countless men overlook or dismiss their value as human beings. Perhaps they have been told they are good for nothing or believed the lies that they were only sperm donors for their children. Many men have low self-esteem. They are vexed by the haunting voices of ghosts from their past failures and never received validation or affirmation from their fathers. These men see themselves as nobodies. Some of these men were molested or sexually assaulted while others have only known the metaphorical chains of poverty. This has robbed them of a true sense of self. These men need God's deliverance to liberate them. They need to know that, although they have flaws, with Divine help they can be good men, husbands, fathers, sons, uncles, and brothers.

Moses went on complaining to God saying, "Who am I that I should go to Pharaoh and bring the Israelites out of Egypt."

(Exodus 3:11) Men often struggle with a lack of identity, having not yet grown into their sense of purpose. They have the biological development of manhood but the mental stagnation of boyhood. Yet God calls boys to become men and one way of maturing us into manhood is by giving us responsibility. Men grow in maturity when given the opportunity to assume the responsibility of surviving in the desert of life, they learn to use their integrity and grit to make it through tough times. Men often learn who they are and what they are made of as a result of the things they experience, the hardships they endure, and the willingness to stand before a Pharaoh on behalf of God.

Moses also protested saying he did not possess sufficient intelligence for the assignment (Exodus 3:13). In many cases, African-American women are better educated and have a higher income than their male counterparts. This can create challenges in pre-marital and marital relationships for men. Standardized testing also unfairly assesses the intelligence levels of minorities. These and other factors cause men to question their intellectual ability to function successfully in higher education. Men are often discouraged by this and settle into roles beneath their true abilities.

Next, Moses argued he did not possess the necessary leadership skills to fulfill the work. Leadership is difficult work and the remaining narrative of Moses' leadership ministry proved to be arduous to say the least. He knew the difference between lordship and leadership. He never attempted to lift himself above God's people but considered himself a servant. He was also a mediator and prayed to God on behalf of the people even when they were in rebellion against Him. Leadership is a privilege and honor to be both taken seriously and enjoyed. The greatest thing a man can be for his family is a servant–leader. He knows where he is leading them and he serves them on the way to the destination.

Persistent in his attempt to get out of doing God's will, Moses claimed his oratorical skills were insufficient to be a spokesman for God before Pharaoh (Exodus 4:10). Moses is merely giving the Lord of a list of excuses of why he is unwilling to fulfill his assignment. Excuses are like armpits, we all have them. The key to overcoming our feelings of inadequacy is to witness and recall the previous times of God's power at work in our lives. Men often make excuses because they feel inadequate for the task at hand. The best thing to do for a man in this position is to pray for him and encourage him; the worst is to berate or belittle him.

Finally, Moses says he is not qualified for the work and God should send someone else (Exodus 4:13). Unfortunately, too many men are saying "let someone else raise my children," "let someone else take care of my needs," "let someone else do the work," and "let someone else take the responsibility." God does not accept our excuses or stubbornness. He still calls men to go and do His will. It is in the process of doing the will of God that men learn to truly trust Him. By maturing through service, men learn that God has the ability to do the job; all He requires is their willingness to accept the responsibility.

Discussion Questions

1. Why does Satan attack men?
2. Why are some men reluctant to lead?
3. What are some ways both women and men can encourage men?
4. In what ways has the discrepancy between the educational level between African-American men and women contributed to relationship challenges?
5. How does a man mature in his faith according to the above material?

Chapter 2

THERE'S A BULL'S-EYE ON A MAN'S BACK

In every system, culture, society, environment, there is a bull's-eye on a man's back. Man was created by God, he is the zenith, the apex, the crown jewel of God's creation. God Jehovah scooped up dust from the ground and made man (Gen. 2:5). However, man was a mannequin until God breathed into his nostrils (pneuma) and he became a living soul (suma). God then equipped man. God loved man above of all His creations. He spent five days creating the heavens and the earth, the universe and the stars, the mountains and the seas, the animals and fowls of the air, and the nocturnal creatures of the night. On the sixth day, He created man. God loved man. He placed him in a utopia, a utopia called the Garden of Eden and provided him with a home, a garden, and food to eat. God provided him with a career, a job as a gardener, and established a meaningful, daily relationship with man. It is because of the deep abiding love God has for man that Satan made man a target.

In Genesis 2:18, God decided it was not good for man to be alone. God became the world's first anesthesiologist and put Adam to sleep. God became the world's first thoracic surgeon and removed a bone from Adam's side. God became the world's first plastic surgeon and closed the flesh up. With that rib from Adam's

4

side, which incidentally is the closest bone to a man's heart, God made woman! (The bone is from his side, as God intended the woman to be side-by-side with the man. Therefore, when a man a gets married, all he does is get his rib back. He should not have any more spare ribs). Due to that relationship, the love that God has for man, the position in which God placed man, he became Satan's public enemy number one. Therefore, Satan devised this nefarious plan for man. He took what God hates, SIN, and put it in what God loves, MAN. Every time God looked at what He loved, MAN, He would also see what He hates: SIN. The devil thought that if God sought to destroy SIN, He would also have to destroy what He loves. Further, the devil thought if God thought to save man whom He loves, He would have to also save the sin that He hates. Despite what the devil thought, God sent Jesus to save man (Matthew 1:21). If He can save you from your sins, He can save you from anything else. He can save you from losing your job, from losing your health, from losing your money, from losing your mind, or even from losing your marriage.

Furthermore, the Pharaoh (Rameses) was fearful when the Hebrews began to grow as a nation under the twelve-tribe system. His advisors, counselors, and consultants informed him that if the Hebrews ever aligned themselves with Egypt's enemies in time of war, Egypt would be at a distinct military disadvantage. To stymie the growth of their nation, the Pharaoh and his advisors decided that Hebrew males could not be allowed to grow up and be powerful solders in the army able to do battle. To ensure this, the Pharaoh issued an edict to the midwives to kill ALL the boy babies. However, God was in the plan; the midwives disregarded the request and baby Moses was spared.

Again we see in Matthew's gospel, at the time of Jesus' birth, the same edict was issued under Herod. Realizing he had been tricked by the wise men who did not return to tell him where the baby Jesus had been born, Herod gave the order to kill all male boys two years old and under. God was in the plan, and Joseph and Mary fled to Egypt for two years during Jesus' infancy.

Discussion Questions

1. Why does God love man?
2. How has the attack against African-Americans continued today?
3. What can women today learn from the midwives, the mother of Moses, and Miriam?
4. How can the church stand against Satan's attack on men?

Chapter 3

SLAVERY AND SEGREGATION'S ATTACK AGAINST MEN

O ur slave heritage as African-American men still has lasting ill-effects on the black race.

Government policies create the absence of black men (much like slavery). Slavery taught us to demean and devalue black women. Slavery left mental, emotional, and psychological scars on black men. There were chains then, now there are jails. There were children born to the unwed then and children born to the unwed now.

The black man was the target. He was sold like cattle, worked like an ox, separated from his family, and psychologically and mentally abused. Slavery targeted the black man.

No laws, caused as much collateral damage as those passed in pursuit of President Lyndon B. Johnson's Great Society, which sought to eliminate poverty by providing housing for the poor, medical care for the young, and attending to the needs of those in poverty.

The notion of taking care of our women and our children only if the male was not present simply provided an incentive to ostracize and emasculate men. This notion also helped to create this staggering figure: 74% of African-American babies are born to single women.

Many people believe that the criminal justice system has massively targeted black men, with disproportionate numbers being arrested and sentenced. The demonization and criminalization of black men and their behavior has led to their disproportionate incarceration rate. Many people also believe that the escalation in police shootings of black males provides further evidence of how man has become targeted.

Discussion Questions

1. How did slavery demean black men?
2. How did slavery divide black families?
3. Do the effects of slavery continue to hurt black families? If so, how?
4. What triggered the Black Lives Matter movement?
5. How has the disparity between the achievements of African-American woman and the lesser achievements of African-American man impacted families?

Chapter 4

THE CHURCH'S ATTACK ON MEN

H ow has the church become a feminine domain? Our actions and activities, ministries, language and terms, education departments, and youth ministries all appear to come from a female angle. The culture within the walls of a church is often effeminate and this culture is often a deterrent to men.

The rise of women in the country and society has sparked and created an atmosphere for the decline of men. The church caters to women. In our language, in our lexicon, and in our verbiage, the church caters to women. Even when we attempt to encourage people to come to Christ, we use female language instead of male language. This may very well be one of the reasons we have significantly more women in church than men. For example, we might say "you need to be in a relationship with Jesus." This is female language. Subconsciously, a man does not want to be "in a relationship" with another man. Better phrases for men might be, "take a walk with Jesus," "take a journey with Jesus," or "be in partnership with Jesus." Men relate more to a fraternity or gang setting. As a matter of fact, the first twelve disciples of Jesus were in a male-exclusive fraternity. I am sure that some of the Galileans, ancient Palestinian people, thought of them as a gang. They fished together, they hunted together, and of course they were with Jesus as He performed miracles. It was a unique fraternity—male-exclusive. Some in the fraternity had some gang tendencies and engaged in gang behavior as we see with the Apostle Peter. He cussed like a sailor and displayed violent tendencies in the Garden of Gethsemane. However, he preached the first sermon on Pentecost.

Discussion Questions

1. In what ways has the church become feminized?
2. Why do so many men fail to see the relevance of the church?
3. What can we do to bring more men back to the church?
4. Why will some men attend church but be reluctant to serve in the church?

Chapter 5

MEN HAVE BOTH VISION AND VICES

1 Corinthians 12:1-10 NOW concerning spiritual gifts, brethren, I do not want you to be ignorant: You know that you were Gentiles, carried away to these dumb idols, however you were led. Therefore I make known to you that no one speaking by the Spirit of God calls Jesus accursed, and no one can say that Jesus is Lord except by the Holy Spirit. There are diversities of gifts, but the same Spirit. There are differences of ministries, but the same Lord. And there are diversities of activities, but it is the same God who works all in all. But the manifestation of the Spirit is given to each one for the profit of all: for to one is given the word of wisdom through the Spirit, to another the word of knowledge through the same Spirit, to another faith by the same Spirit, to another gifts of healings by the same Spirit, to another the working of miracles, to another prophecy, to another discerning of spirits, to another different kinds of tongues, to another the interpretation of tongues. But one and the same Spirit works all these things, distributing to each one individually as He wills. For as the body is one and has many members, but all the members of that one body, being many, are one body, so also is Christ.

In our prior studies regarding the struggles experienced by men we determined a large number of men struggle in the areas of money, women, and power. This present passage provides us with an ancient look at men in the regions of Achaia and into the life of one of God's greatest men, the Apostle Paul. In many ways, Paul provided a portrait for all godly men to hang in the corridors of their minds as a pattern to follow.

Paul was in every sense of the word a man. He was intelligent. He was artistic. He was a hard worker. He made a positive difference in the world. He was tough. He took a lickin' and kept on tickin'. He lived with purpose. He was deeply spiritual and radically religious. He walked by faith and not by sight. Although he walked in the flesh, he did not war after the flesh. The weapons of his warfare were not carnal. Instead, they were mighty through God in order to pull down strongholds and cast down imaginations and all high things that exalted themselves against the knowledge of God.

Paul was a man both of the word and his word. He was gifted in the miraculous, yet he remained humble. He fought against God, then fought for God. He put people in prison and he spent time in prison. He was the chief of sinners, but he obtained grace and mercy. Paul was a man's man in the sense that he could relate to men on all levels of life.

Paul could stand before rulers and roughnecks. He could communicate with Festus and felons. He could motivate men and inspire passion. He learned to be content in whatsoever state he was in. He was crucified with Christ, yet Christ lived in him. Paul could articulate the Gospel and explain salvation. He could rightly divide the Scripture. He was intensely thoughtful and theological. In speaking of Paul, Peter said, "As also in all his epistles, speaking in them of these things; in which are some things hard to understand, which untaught and unstable people twist to their own destruction, as they do also the rest of the Scriptures." (2 Pet. 3:16)

In appearance, Paul was not impressive. "For his letters, they say are weighty and powerful, but his bodily presence is weak, and his speech contemptible." 2 Cor. 10:10). Like many men, he found himself in a defensive posture. The false-teaching Judaizers called him out. Paul had to defend his apostolic authority as God's man. In essence, Paul said (make no bones about it): "I am a man of God." He said, "I'll let you know how much of a man I really am!" In comparing himself to his opponents, listen to what Paul put forth!

"What! Do you not have houses to eat and drink in? Or do you despise the church of God and shame those who have nothing? What shall I say to you? Shall I praise you in this? I do not praise you. For I received from the Lord that which I also delivered to you: that the Lord Jesus on the same night in which He was betrayed took bread; and when He had given thanks, He broke it and said, "Take, eat; this is My body which is broken for you; do this in remembrance of Me." In the same manner He also took the cup after supper, saying, "This cup is the new covenant in My blood. This do, as often as you drink it, in remembrance of Me." For as often as you eat this bread and drink this cup, you proclaim the Lord's death till He comes. Therefore whoever eats this bread or drinks this cup of the Lord in an unworthy manner will be guilty of the body and blood of the Lord. But let a man examine himself, and so let him eat of the bread and drink of the cup. For he who eats and drinks in an unworthy manner eats and drinks judgment to himself, not discerning the Lord's body" (2 Corinthians 11:22-29)

Paul proved himself to be God's man. However, he again said "who is weak, and I am not weak?" In other words, he was weak just as others were weak. He appeared strong based on all that he had been through, yet he professed to be weak. He didn't want to boast about his accomplishments. He didn't want to draw attention to himself because he didn't want to detract from God's glory.

Our families, churches, and communities need more strong men like the Apostle Paul. We need men with muscle and minds, with bronze and brains, with endurance and eternal life. We need men with force and faith, with power and praise, with work and worship. We need men with strength and Scripture.

The key to Paul's manhood was his weakness. It was not his ability, but God's ability, not his wisdom, but God's wisdom. In order to be a strong man of God, you must first embrace your weakness, you must embrace the genuineness of your own limitations. The requirements and demands of being a man in today's world will crush you like a boulder if you do not accept your weakness. You are not Atlas and you cannot hold the entire world on your shoulders. As a man, there is substantial pressures and demands on you from many directions. You are expected to be the leader and provider in the home. Your wife sees you as Prince Charming while the children expect you to be like the dad portrayed by Will Smith in *The Pursuit of Happiness*. Your career and vocation is increasingly demanding, your employers want more of your time and energy at the same pay while you see other less experienced men come and receive promotions with higher pay and more benefits. You are expected to be a handyman with *MacGyver*-type skills able to repair anything in the house or garage. Yet at the same time, you are being pressured by the temptation to escape your world by finding some type of oasis to which you can escape from your desert. You are unhappy. You love your family. You are grateful for your job.

You are giving them what they need, but you are having trouble giving them what they want. You are giving them things when what they really want is you. Your wife wants you to truly communicate with her, to open yourself up to her, but you are not sure how to do it without sounding weak. She is really not concerned with scores, hoops, homeruns, RBI's, and slam dunks. Your children would rather have your presence than your presents. They want the security of your love and the validation of your acceptance.

Part of the problem is men often fail to develop a healthy sense of masculine identity, they fail to recognize their spirituality and investigate their God-given spiritual resources. When you are able to recognize and embrace your weaknesses and limitations as a man, you are well on your way to unlocking the key to your success as a man.

"For you see your calling, brethren, that not many wise according to the flesh, not many mighty, not many noble, are called. But God has chosen the foolish things of the world to put to shame the wise, and God has chosen the weak things of the world to put to shame the things which are mighty; and the base things of the world and the things which are despised God has chosen, and the things which are not, to bring to nothing the things that are, that no flesh should glory in His presence" (1 Cor. 1:26-29).

The Vision of Paradise

"It is doubtless not profitable for me to boast. I will come to visions and revelations of the Lord: I know a man in Christ who fourteen years ago—whether in the body I do not know, or whether out of the body I do not know, God knows—such a one was caught up to the third heaven. And I know such a man—whether in the body or out of the body I do not know, God knows—how he was caught up into Paradise and heard inexpressible words, which it is not lawful for a man to utter. Of such a one I will boast; yet of myself I will not boast, except in my infirmities. For though I might desire to boast, I will not be a fool; for I will speak the truth. But I refrain, lest anyone should think of me above what he sees me to be or hears from me."(2 Cor. 12:1-6)

Paul had spoken of being let down in a basket through a window, but then he spoke of being caught up to the third heaven. The first describes protection and the latter describes privilege. Paul was spared for a purpose. In his weakness, he could not protect himself from his enemies. He recognized God's hand interwoven into the very fabric of his life and circumstances.

It is with great restraint that Paul even mentioned this vision of paradise. The false teachers who were opposing him forced him to it. Paul described an experience of paradise fourteen years prior to this writing. Unquestionable, Paul was the man being referred to, he was a man of many visions and revelations which the Lord had given him, revelations concerning the mysteries of God.

- Vision of Jesus on the Damascus Road (Acts 9:3)
- Vision of Ananias coming to him (Acts 9:12)
- Vision to minister to the Gentiles (Acts 22:17)
- Vision of Macedonia (Acts 16:9)
- Vision of encouragement (Acts 18:9-10)
- Vision of encouragement (Acts 23:11)
- Vision of the angel of God (Acts 27:23)

This vision of being caught up into the third heaven is by far the greatest vision Paul ever experienced. It was so wonderful, he could not fully describe this event. He could not say if he went in body or out of body for only God knows. While he was there, he heard unrepeatable words not lawful for a man to utter. It was wonderful, but he could not tell anyone about it.

The "third heaven" and "paradise" are synonyms. Heaven is the Greek term *ouranos*, which means the abode of God. The area of the sky from which the rain and wind come would be the first heaven. The second heaven would be the area of the sun, moon, and stars. Paradise is *paradeisos*; it is a word with Persian roots depicting a park or an Eden (place of future happiness). Every man needs a vision of paradise for himself and his family. If the blind lead the blind, they both fall into the ditch. People perish where there is no vision, so men need a vision for the future of their families, they need to think of the generations to come after them. The vision does not have to be lofty or materialistic, it can be a vision of perpetuating family faith, love, integrity, hard work, or unity.

Paul's vision of paradise can be a great help to men of today. It was Paul's vision from God that made him stand out among other men. Any man willing to accept God's call on his life has the same opportunity to stand out among men. Certainly if Paul was not sufficient in himself to escape the governor of Damascus, even more so he was not sufficient in himself to be lifted up to the third heaven in the physical sense. Men, there are some places you cannot escape without God's help and there are some places you cannot reach without God's help. A vision of paradise gives a man direction and clarity. It helps him to understand the spiritual is far superior to the temporal. Men, do not allow your greatness to die with you. Leave a legacy for your future generations. A vision of paradise helps a man appreciate what is categorically important, helps a man reorganize his life's priorities so "first things really do come first."

"**Vision... is a *clear mental image* of a *preferable future imparted by God* to *His chosen servants,* and is based upon an *accurate understanding* of God, self, and circumstances.**"

The Vice of Pain

"And lest I should be exalted above measure by the abundance of the revelations, a thorn in the flesh was given to me, a messenger of Satan to buffet me, lest I be exalted above measure. Concerning this thing I pleaded with the Lord three times that it might depart from me." (2 Corinthians 12:7-8)

In order to prevent the apostle from being lifted up in pride, the Lord allowed a messenger of Satan to buffet him. Buffet literally means "to rap with the fist." The idea of this passage is one of constant or frequent buffeting.

Paul called this "a thorn in the flesh." There is no definitive answer to the exact nature of this thorn in the flesh. It was real, it was physical, and it caused Paul much pain. It grieved him so that he prayed to the Lord three times for it to depart. In life, we have both paradise and pain, we experience both treasure and trial.

There are many theories about Paul's thorn in the flesh: epilepsy, hysteria, neuralgia, depression, visual deficits, malaria, leprosy, rheumatism, a speech impediment, temptation, and personal enemies.

Today's man must be able to endure the vice of pain. Every man must be willing to accept his "thorn in the flesh." Some men suffer in silence: they feel uncomfortable being vulnerable with others and do not want to appear weak. They are trained to be tough and withhold their emotions. Men do not usually verbalize their love to their wives and children because they never saw it modeled by the men in their own lives. Like all human beings, men suffer from anxiety, depression, stress, post-traumatic stress disorder, abuse, and some men have actually been raped by or molested by both men and women, but these are things not usually discussed. Men experience various hurts such as grief, unresolved trauma, loneliness, and feelings of inadequacy. Minority men are especially prone to develop maladaptive methods of coping with their pain, hurts, disappointments, and hunger for the father they never knew.

And as a result of these underlining pains, men are susceptible to developing dangerous vices and habits to cope with an agony too ugly to face. I am not suggesting Paul is exhibiting or describing any immoral vices of his own. However, many men suffer in silence with their vices such as anger, resentment, bitterness, alcoholism, domestic violence, child abuse, drug abuse, violent crimes, and gang activity. Unlike Paul, we do not pray for God to remove our thorns. We do not ask Him to remove the vices we use to cope with the disappointments and dejections. We become convinced we have no other alternative than to live with the thorn even though it causes excruciating pain to both our bodies and our spirits. Therefore, many of us suffer in silence. We wear the masks of our public persona, saying everything is great, but there may be a deep, empty hole within. But the overwhelming goodness that is God allows us to be buffeted so we will not be exalted beyond measure. God allows Satan to mess with us but not murder us. It is a great paradox. God often responds to men in the same way as He responded to Paul. The Lord denies our request to remove the thorn, He refuses to pull Satan back. God knows something about men we can only discover when we have experienced the brutality of being buffeted by Satan. The Lord does not need to remove our thorns of hurt, frustration, overworked, or feeling our cries for support go unanswered, and seething with resentment at the disrespect we endure. But the struggles continue: sick children, challenging jobs that drain us, spiritual apathy, troubled marriages, and churches that ignore our genuine needs for validation and affirmation. Left untreated, these experiences become incarcerating vices, locking men behind the doors of depravities such as pornography, profanity, promiscuity, and poverty.

But these doors can be unlocked, the chains can be broken. It is not as simple as Paul and Silas praying and praising their way out of prison.[1] The Lord can do anything but fail. However, he refuses this humble plea to remove the thorn and to take away the pain because there is a greater purpose at work.

Men have a propensity to allow their success in the workplace and their exterior persona of status, titles, conquests, and bank accounts to define them. But the Lord knows these tendencies in men will lead to something more severe than a thorn in the flesh. One of the first things men must accept is our own humanity and the Lord's Deity. When we accept this basic theological truth, we are now on our way to learning to live with the pain and lean into the discomfort of our personal thorns. Life in this world is not intended to go perfectly. We will experience tribulation in the

---

[1] Acts 16:25-34.

19

world.[2] You will experience pain: health can be taken away, family ripped apart, material possessions lost, jobs phased out.

You will have some "thorns in the flesh." Your wife may become grievously ill or a child may go astray. Some loved ones will leave or some of the people you thought were your friends will turn their backs on you. Business partners may try to cheat you and investments may go south. The economy may collapse and war may erupt.

The messenger of Satan is still on the prowl, seeking what men he can devour. Don't think for one minute you will live without opposition or challenges. Just believe God is bigger than any challenge you can ever face.

During a men's workshop, one hundred Christian men were randomly and anonymously surveyed. These men were diverse in ethnicity, marital status, age, and economic status. These men love the Lord. They love their families. They serve in the Lord's church, but were willing to be transparent regarding their vices. Their main faults and vices included insecurity, fear, poor health, money, pornography, lust, fornication and adultery. The Lord cannot heal our wounds as long as we continue to ignore them. While some may find this appalling and disturbing, it reflects some of the realities we need to face as we minister to both men and our churches. Furthermore, our intent is not to destroy these men or any other believer overtaken by a fault but to help restore them.[3]

The Victory of Power

And he said unto me, my grace is sufficient for thee: for my strength is made perfect in weakness. Most gladly therefore will I rather glory in my infirmities, that the power of Christ may rest

---

[2] John 16:33

[3] Galatians 6:1-4

upon me. Therefore I take pleasure in infirmities, in reproaches, in necessities, in persecutions, in distresses for Christ's sake: for when I am weak, then am I strong. (2 Cor. 12:9-10)

Paul spoke here of the victory of power through a paradoxical statement. Paul recognized his limitations. He was unable to rid himself of his thorn but his pain pushed him to prayer. Men cannot obtain the wisdom, strength, or grace to be healed from their brokenness and wounds by calling on the Lord for help. The Lord's grace is sufficient unto all afflictions and He responds to us with that grace just as He responded to Paul. Grace is God's provision for our needs when we do not deserve it.

His grace is sufficient. *It is sufficient for our ministries.* "Not that we are sufficient of ourselves to think anything as of ourselves; but our sufficiency is of God." (2 Cor. 3:5) *His grace is sufficient for our material needs.* "And God is able to make all grace abound toward you; that ye, always having all sufficiency in all things, may abound to every good work." (2 Cor. 8:9)

His grace is strengthening. Literally, Paul stated through his own weakness he is continuously receiving God's power. It was his weakness that made him strong. Apart from Christ, a man cannot be everything for his family, church, and community. The power is of Christ and not of men.

Paul chose to most gladly glory in his infirmities or weakness because he wanted the power of God to rest upon him. "Rest upon him" literally means "tent upon him." He wanted the power of Christ to be like a covering for him.

Do not make the mistake of asking for substitutions, because what we need is transformation. Paul wanted the Lord to substitute his thorn with comfort, yet ultimately what he received was transformation. When God told him to deal with the thorn, Paul had to transform his thinking about the thorn. Stop looking for explanations and start looking for God's promises to help endure the thorns.

Grace gives our weakness access to His power, which makes us strong. God did not change Paul's situation; He just added grace. Strong Men Are Really Weak. When it is your power, you receive the glory, but when it is His power, He receives the glory.

Discussion Questions

1. How can a wife support her husband's vision for their family?
2. What does is it mean for a wife to be her husband's helper? (Gen. 2)
3. Why will God hinder prayer? (1 Pet. 3:1-7)
4. How do Christians restore men overtaken by a fault or struggling with a vice?

Chapter 6

WHERE ARE THE MEN GOD CREATED?

Genesis 3:6-12

So when the woman saw that the tree was good for food, that it was pleasant to the eyes, and a tree desirable to make one wise, she took of its fruit and ate. She also gave to her husband with her, and he ate. Then the eyes of both of them were opened, and they knew that they were naked; and they sewed fig leaves together and made themselves coverings. And they heard the sound of the LORD God walking in the garden in the cool of the day, and Adam and his wife hid themselves from the presence of the LORD God among the trees of the garden. Then the LORD God called to Adam and said to him, "Where are you?" So he said, "I heard Your voice in the garden, and I was afraid because I was naked; and I hid myself." And He said, "Who told you that you were naked? Have you eaten from the tree of which I commanded you that you should not eat?" Then the man said, "The woman whom You gave to be with me, she gave me of the tree, and I ate." NKJV

God is the Creator. At His divine initiative and by His own prerogative, the Lord stood in the vastness of eternity and spoke time into existence. Clearly, Moses, the great lawgiver, wanted us to recognize that Creation is the work of God. When he communicates the history concerning the seven days of Creation, he makes it overwhelmingly clear that God is the agent.

God acts alone in Creation. The subject and verb combination is categorically cohesive. In Genesis 1 and 2, we find this agreement. God said. God saw. God called. God made. God created. God blessed. God rested. God formed. God planted. God took and put. God caused. God took and closed up. God brought.

Creation is central to our existence and faith. In fact, the Scriptures begin by giving us a history of Creation. Furthermore, the Scriptures end with a description of a new heaven and a new earth.

As they confessed to and worshipped the Lord their God for removing their reproach, the people during the days of Nehemiah stood up and blessed the glorious name of God exalted above all blessing and praise. They said, "You alone are the LORD; You have made heaven, The heaven of heavens, with all their host, The earth and everything on it, The seas and all that is in them, And You preserve them all. The host of heaven worships You. ." (Neh. 9:6)

The Psalmist described the Lord's eternal love as he offered a prayer for the afflicted when they were overwhelmed and cried out with their complaints. The Psalmist wrote, "Of old You laid the foundation of the earth, And the heavens are the work of Your hands. They will perish, but You will endure; Yes, they will all grow old like a garment; Like a cloak You will change them, And they will be changed. But You are the same, And Your years will have no end. The children of Your servants will continue, And their descendants will be established before You." (Ps. 102:25-28)

Creation is the root of righteousness. During the spiritually dilapidated days of Isaiah, the Lord said through the prophet:

> For thus says the LORD, Who created the heavens,
> Who is God, Who formed the earth and made it,
> Who has established it. Who did not create it in

vain, Who formed it to be inhabited: I am the
LORD, and there is no other. I have not spoken in
secret, in a dark place of the earth; I did not say to
the seed of Jacob, 'seek Me in vain'; I, the LORD,
speak righteousness, I declare things that are right.
(Isa. 45:18-19)

God created men. The gender distinction between men and
women is a product of God's creation. God created men first.
When the LORD God formed man of the dust of the ground, He
breathed into his nostrils the breath of life and man became a living
being (Gen 2:7). God created man in His own image and likeness.

God created man because there was no man to till the ground
(Gen. 2:6). The LORD God put the man in the Garden of Eden to
tend and keep it (Gen. 2:15). Furthermore, the LORD God gave
the man specific instructions to eat freely from all the trees of
Garden except the tree of the knowledge of good and evil (Gen.
2:17), "for in the day that you eat of it you shall surely die."

God gave the man a wife as a suitable helper in the word and
the work of God. She was taken from his rib with divine assistance while he slept. God made this woman! God brought her to
the man. Adam rejoiced and declared "bone of my bones and flesh
of my flesh" (Gen 2:23). As they were joined together, they were
not ashamed.

God created men. He created men with dignity and dominion
and endowed them with great potential. He equipped them with
the tools and talents to achieve the divine purpose. God created
men to be servant-leaders. God gave men His word and work
before He gave him a wife. Adam had no human role models.
He had no larger-than-life personalities to admire and compare
himself to. Adam had no earthly father to teach him about being
a husband and father. Adam had no grandfather, uncle, brother,
preacher, elder, deacon, or fellow brother to serve as a role model.

The Lord served as Adam's role model! The Lord gave him the word. He gave him the power of life and death. He did not learn about manhood from Esquire or GQ magazine. God created him to follow instructions. He was created to act in faithful obedience to God's word. *For all of the men that never had positive role models, you need to understand God is the perfect role model.* If you follow the Lord's example and word, you will be a real man.

We must understand, however, that from all indications God created Adam fully grown. Adam did not have a mother. Adam was not conceived in a woman's womb. There is no indication that Adam was ever an infant, toddler, or preschooler. There is no indication that Adam ever went through the teenage years of adolescence.

An infant with the XY chromosomes is not a man at birth. He is called and created to become a man. Paul wanted us to understand there is a distinction between a child and a man. Paul said, "When I was a child, I spoke as a child, understood as a child, I thought as a child; but when I became a man, I put away childish things" (1 Cor. 13:11). He was born a child, but he became a man. When did he become a man? Although he was Jewish, Paul did not mention his bar mitzvah as his rite of passage into manhood. He did not become a man when he stopped speaking, understanding, and thinking like a child. **He became a man when he put away childish things!**

Someone said the only difference between boys and men is the cost of their toys.

Boys love bicycles; men love motorcycles.

Boys love hot wheels; men love hot rods.

Boys play with toy trucks; men play with monster trucks.

Boys build with Lego; men build with wood, iron, and steel.

Boys play with girls; men play with women.

Do not underestimate the importance of Creation in understanding manhood and womanhood as comparable companions rather than simply egalitarian equivalents. There has been a persistent effort to demolish the divine decree regarding men and women. However, few actively engaged on the frontlines of this movement have accurately considered Creation.

Jesus went back to Creation when the Pharisees tested him by asking is it lawful for a man to divorce his wife for any reason (Matt. 19:3-6). The Lord replied by quoting Genesis 1:27 and 2:24. When addressing the Ephesians about the role of women in the church, Paul said, "for Adam was formed first, then Eve" (1 Tim. 2:13).

What happened to the men God created? Why does it appear that so many with the XY chromosomes are in suspended animation or arrested development? Why are so few men in church? Why are so many men involved in drugs and gangs? Why are so few men graduating high school and attending college? Why are so many men victims of violence? Why are so many men incarcerated? Why are there so many Desmond Hatchetts out there? Mr. Hatchett is the man from Knoxville, TN who has twenty-one children by eleven different women. Desmond is only twenty-nine years old and the children are all between the ages of newborn and eleven years old. In addition, he makes minimum wage.

Adam gives us insight in answering this question from a biblical perspective. There are many psychological, socio-economic, philosophical, and political factors contributing to the problems and challenges faced by men. There is something underneath these factors. It is not merely a social problem, a race problem, an injustice problem, or a philosophical problem. It is a spiritual problem rooted in a denial of God and disobedience to God.

In other words, a growing number of people no longer consider God or His word as authoritative in their lives. Dr. David F. Wells postulated that the Church has abandoned the transcendent word of God. According to Wells, this led the Church to look to the self for a substitute word. It has assigned to the self all the tasks that biblical authority once exercised. Today, many count the self as their only authority.[2]

When I look to a distorted sense of self, it compounds the problem. The prominent scholar Dr. W.E.B. Du Bois described this self-distortion in African-Americans as a double-consciousness:

> ...the Negro is a sort of seventh son, born with a veil, and gifted with second-sight in this American world, a world which yields him no true self-consciousness, but only lets him see through the revelation of the other world. It is a peculiar sensation, this double-consciousness, this sense of always looking at one's self through the eyes of others, of measuring one's soul by the tape of a world that looks on in amused contempt and pity. One ever feels his twoness: an American, a Negro; two souls, two thoughts, two unreconciled strivings; two warring ideals in one dark body, whose dogged strength alone keeps it from being torn asunder.[3]

Scholar and theologian Dr. James H. Cone described Malcolm X's struggle with self-definition in his formative years. "With no parental love to affirm his personhood (father killed and mother locked away) and to instill in him the self-confidence that he was as good as anybody else, he, though gifted and popular, did not have the emotional strength to cope with a white society that refused to recognize his humanity."[4]

The Woman's Assertion

"So when the woman saw that the tree was good for food, that it was pleasant to the eyes, and a tree desirable to make one wise, she took of its fruit and ate. She also gave to her husband with her, and he ate." (Gen. 3:6)

It is impossible to completely understand what is happening with men without considering what is happening with women. Eve stepped outside of and violated her role. She stepped out of her lane. She became the pilot and usurped Adam's leadership.

Her assignment was to help Adam in fulfilling God's word and doing God's work. Evidently, she was dissatisfied with her role as helper and assumed action as the head. It is important to understand Eve did not make this decision because of financial distress. She was not being abused or unjustly treated. There were no such things as equal rights. There was no indication of boredom or tiredness from childcare. Eve was not oppressed.

She made an independent decision and defied God by assuming headship over Adam. Eve wanted to be in charge and she took over. She wanted to wear the pants (so to speak) and no longer wanted to follow. She thought this would help the family. Later she would say, *"The serpent deceived me, and I ate"*(Gen 3:13). In Hebrew, this is *nasha' (naw-shaw')*, which means to lead astray, to delude, to seduce, or to beguile.[5]

By her own admission, the serpent deceived her. She believed his lie. She doubted and then defied God's word. She wanted to seize power or authority in becoming like God. Instead of appreciating God for being able to freely eat from the trees of the garden, she focused on the one limitation, rule, or restriction. This focus and sense of dissatisfaction often leads women to assert themselves concerning men.

There is a difference between taking power and being empowered.

There is a difference between control and cooperation.
There is a difference between leadership and followship.
There is a difference between roles and goals.
There is a difference between headship and submission.
There is a difference between self-will and God's will.
There is a difference between taking over and teamwork.
There is a difference between responding and initiating.

African-American slavery produced a similar spirit among women as did the liberation and feminist movements, but for different reasons. It is the same result, but it has different grounds. One was launched because of political oppression (right to vote). The other was launched by physical and social oppression. African-American slavery created a matriarchal family structure and undermined the role and authority of the husband.

The Man's Abdication

"Then the eyes of both of them were opened, and they knew that they were naked; and they sewed fig leaves together and made themselves coverings. And they heard the sound of the LORD God walking in the garden in the cool of the day, and Adam and his wife hid themselves from the presence of the LORD God among the trees of the garden." (Gen. 3:7-8)

Now Adam and Eve were in the same condition. For both of them, their eyes were opened, they knew they were naked. Both had sewn fig leaves and made themselves coverings. Then they heard the sound of the Lord God walking in the cool of the day and they both hid themselves from His presence among the trees of the garden.

Yes, the woman was assertive, she did assume leadership. But they were in this condition because Adam, the man, abdicated his responsibility. Listen to Paul on this issue. Paul said, "Therefore, just as through one man sin entered the world, and death through sin, and thus death spread to all men, because all sinned." (Rom. 5:12) Sin came into the world through Adam.

Adam was not deceived when he ate (1 Tim. 2:14). He knowingly disobeyed God. The Lord created him with dignity and dominion and gave him headship and leadership. The Lord furnished him with the word of life and death and gave him talents, gifts, and abilities. The Lord gave him the Garden of Eden and a wife. However, when it came to the forbidden fruit, the Lord did not give it to him; his wife gave it to him.

He abdicated his responsibility and now they were both naked and hiding from God among the trees. Too many men are abdicating their roles and responsibilities. The Lord expects men to fulfill their roles and responsibilities. God expected Adam to carry out His will and work. The Lord judged Eli along with his house forever because he knew of his sons' iniquity, but he did not restrain them and their vileness (1 Sam. 3:13). Too many men are abdicating their role and responsibilities.

Too many preachers are not preaching the word.

Too many elders are not shepherding the flock.

Too many deacons are not serving the people.

Too many husbands are not leading and caring for their wives.

Too many fathers are not parenting their children.

Too many sons are not respecting and caring for their families.

Too many brethren are not being faithful to the Lord.

Too many Christians are not fulfilling their roles as salt and light.

The Participant's Accountability

"Then the LORD God called to Adam and said to him, "Where are you?" So he said, "I heard Your voice in the garden, and I was afraid because I was naked; and I hid myself." And He said, "Who

31

told you that you were naked? Have you eaten from the tree of which I commanded you that you should not eat?" Then the man said, "The woman whom You gave to be with me, she gave me of the tree, and I ate." And the LORD God said to the woman, "What is this you have done?" The woman said, "The serpent deceived me, and I ate." (Gen. 3:9-13)

The Lord called all of the parties to account for their actions. The Lord addressed the man, the woman, and the serpent. God asked several questions in this passage. He asked both the man and woman some questions, but he did not ask the serpent any questions.

To Adam, God said, **"Where are you?"** Now these are all rhetorical questions. Everyone already knows the answers. It is like when a parent or spouse calls you to question for something they already know, but you are not sure they know. However, you suspect by the fact that they asked the question something is up. The Lord is omniscient. He knows everything. He knows our thoughts before we think them. He knows the number of hairs on our head. He calls all the stars by name. He knows the actual and the possible. The Lord knows when no one else knows.

The serpent talked to the woman. However, the LORD talked to the man. Where are you? I left you in charge. I gave you my word. I was clear in my communication and expectation. Why did you let the serpent near your wife? Why did you eat from the tree?

Look at yourself now. You are a hot mess. You and your woman are hiding among the trees with fig leaf coverings. Before you ate, you were naked and not ashamed (Gen 2:25). Now your eyes are opened. You do not see yourselves in the same way anymore. Sin has created a sense of shame.

We sin by commission and omission. We must understand the unity between the worship (word) of the Church and the work of the Church. We have made them separate issues. It is true that we cannot get some men to participate in the worship of the church.

However, it is also true that we can get fewer men to participate in the work of the church.

In recent years, we have put significant emphasis on church worship to the exclusion of the work of the church but both are required of God's people. Thank God we have numerous brethren for worship participation. Yet, where are you when it comes to the work of the church?

Where are you when it **comes to ministry**?

Where are you when God needs van drivers?

Where are you when God needs the sick to be visited?

Where are you when we need the doors opened and closed?

Where are you when God needs grass to be mowed?

Where are you when God needs evangelism classes to be taught?

Where are you when God needs laborers for His vineyard?

Where are you when it comes to actually being involved beyond worship?

The Lord's Atonement is the final piece. "Also for Adam and his wife the LORD God made tunics of skin, and clothed them. " (Gen. 3:21) After the Lord cursed the serpent and the ground, He meted out consequences for the man and the woman. The Lord did not curse the woman or the man because He had already blessed them. Watch the Lord's saving and amazing grace.

Previously, they attempted to cover their own nakedness with fig leaves. So many times we try to cover our shame and nakedness. We hide from God's presence out of fear. Yet God comes walking in the cool of the garden. He comes looking for us. He comes not to condemn us, but to save us. He comes to redeem us. He comes to restore us. He comes to renew us. He comes to cover our sin. He comes to reconcile us.

Discussion Questions

1. Why do some men give in to their wives?
2. Why did Satan speak to Eve rather than Adam?
3. Who did God assign leadership to in the relationship between Adam and Eve?
4. Who suffered consequences as a result of the Fall and how did it affect their relationship?

Chapter 7

MEN FOR MINISTRY

Acts 6:1-7

N ow in those days, when the number of the disciples was multiplying, there arose a complaint against the Hebrews by the Hellenists, because their widows were neglected in the daily distribution. Then the twelve summoned the multitude of the disciples and said, "It is not desirable that we should leave the word of God and serve tables. Therefore, brethren, seek out from among you seven men of good reputation, full of the Holy Spirit and wisdom, whom we may appoint over this business; but we will give ourselves continually to prayer and to the ministry of the word." And the saying pleased the whole multitude. And they chose Stephen, a man full of faith and the Holy Spirit, and Philip, Prochorus, Nicanor, Timon, Parmenas, and Nicolas, a proselyte from Antioch, whom they set before the apostles; and when they had prayed, they laid hands on them. Then the word of God spread, and the number of the disciples multiplied greatly in Jerusalem, and a great many of the priests were obedient to the faith.

The Jerusalem church was growing. On the day of inception, three thousand souls were added (Acts 2:41). It was an explosive growth because every day the Lord added to the church those who were being saved (Acts 2:47). Luke stated the number of saved men who responded to the Gospel preaching of Peter and John was five thousand (Acts 4:4). Luke also said "And believers were increasingly added to the Lord, multitudes of both men and women" (Acts 5:14).

The Church was growing. People recognized their unfinished and lost conditions. Those who heard the Gospel were pierced in their hearts. Those who were hungry and thirsty for salvation asked, "what must I do to be saved?" Those who gladly received the word repented and were baptized. They were immersed in water for the remission of sins.

The church was growing, but the enemy was "seeking whom he may devour." The enemy had previously attacked the church with painful persecution (Acts 4:1-31; 5:17-41). Yet this persecution actually accelerated growth. The enemy filled the heart of Ananias to lie to the Holy Spirit. Today the enemy attacks through dissension in the church.

The rapid growth of the church ultimately led to a problem. Growing churches must be prepared to respond to the increased and diverse needs of the people. When people are saved, they often have both identified and unidentified problems that need to be addressed.

The church must be organized to meet the growing needs of the people. As the church grows, so does every facet of the church: the ministry, fellowship, and life. When there is an action, there will be a reaction. The passage above is vital in understanding the need for structure and mutual love among the people of God. As we organize this church with elders and deacons, this text gives us a theological and practical framework to assess and implement.

The Complaint

> Now in those days, when the number of the disciples was multiplying, there arose a complaint

against the Hebrews by the Hellenists, because
their widows were neglected in the daily distribution. (Acts 6:1) NKJV

The Hellenists were not native or Palestinian Hebrews. A
Hellenist was a Jew by birth or religion. They spoke Greek rather
than Aramaic or Hebrew. They studied from the Greek transla-
tion of the Old Testament known as the Septuagint rather than
the Hebrew Scriptures. The Hellenists also included proselytes,
regardless of whether they converted to Christianity. The Pharisees
considered them to be second-class Jews[6]

The Hellenists were complaining. They were grumbling with
discontent because their widows were being neglected and slighted
in the daily ministration of alms and not receiving the same com-
passionate love as the Hebrew widows.

The care of widows was not new to Christianity. The Law
taught to care for the needy; this included the widow (Deut. 14:29;
16:11; 24:19-21; 26:12). The Lord said:

When you reap your harvest in your field, and forget a sheaf
in the field, you shall not go back to get it; it shall be for the
stranger, the fatherless, and the widow, that the Lord your God
may bless you in all the work of your hands. When you beat your
olive trees, you shall not go over the boughs again; it shall be for
the stranger, the fatherless, and the widow. When you gather the
grapes of your vineyard, you shall not glean it afterward; it shall
be for the stranger, the fatherless, and the widow. And you shall
remember that you were a slave in the land of Egypt; therefore I
command you to do this thing. (Deut. 24:19-22). NKJV

This was the command to the individual in the Old Testament.
However, we must understand the significance of the widow from
1 Timothy 5:3-16. The IRS says benevolence can only be given for
food, medical emergencies, housing, clothing, and utilities.

However, in this case, these Hellenists widows were in significant need. They were not receiving loving care and justice. They were being neglected and overlooked. When they came to the church looking for Christ, they experienced a cruel crisis. Furthermore, the Hellenist Jews were being neglected on purpose.

The Challenge

> Then the twelve summoned the multitude of the disciples and said, it is not desirable that we should leave the word of God and serve tables. Therefore, brethren, seek out from among you seven men of good reputation, full of the Holy Spirit and wisdom, whom we may appoint over this business; but we will give ourselves continually to prayer and to the ministry of the word. (Acts 6:2-4)

Complaints often lead to challenge when there is no organization in place to maintain equilibrium, balance, and homeostasis. Leadership must be able to deal with the challenges of the church. This was not a challenge for just the twelve. It was the challenge for the entire church.

The twelve called a congregational meeting. **"It is not desirable that we should leave the word of God and serve tables."** Today's church is in trouble because those entrusted with proclaiming the word and feeding the flock are serving tables. It has been commonly reported that the preachers are doing elders' work, elders are doing deacons' work, and deacons don't know what to do.

The church will stop growing if the twelve men of God abandon the word of God and prayer in order to serve tables. Many leaders are frustrated and burnt out because they are stuck serving tables. Now the tables must be served. Serving tables is honorable and necessary. The church cannot grow and function at optimal health if the tables are not served.

The twelve apostles evaluated the situation and determined the solution to this important challenge was to increase the size of the workforce. The answer was not to distract or give the twelve more to do. The answer was **"brethren, seek out from among you seven men."** As a team, these men would work together in solving critical problems.

The additional leaders and workers were to be men from among the church. Here is the challenge today. Most congregations can not grow because the men are **unable, unwilling,** or **unavailable** to serve tables.

Some believe these seven men were deacons. They may have had similarities with deacons, but I do not believe they were deacons in an official sense. Luke mentioned elders, but he never mentioned deacons.

Notice what qualities were used to identify these men. They had to be seven men of **good reputation.** The original term appears like the English word "mature." It means to be well testified about and to be lauded. They were to be above reproach. They were to be men of integrity with honest reports.

The potential candidates to serve in the capacity of resolving the disputes regarding the neglect of the Hellenist Jews had to be full of the **Holy Spirit.** They had to be under the guidance of the Holy Spirit. They must have yielded to the Holy Spirit. They must have been sealed with the Holy Spirit. They must have demonstrated the fruit of the Holy Spirit.

They had to be full of wisdom. Wisdom or 'Sophia' means skilled in the affairs of life, practical wisdom, wise management as shown in forming the best plans and selecting the best means, including the idea of sound judgment and good sense.

The twelve would appoint these seven men to this business or responsibility of caring for the widows. When reading and studying the text, a question arose about how the distribution was being conducted before this appointment. Who was responsible prior to this appointment?

The twelve were now free to continually give themselves to prayer and the ministry of the word.

The Choice

> And the saying pleased the whole multitude. And they chose Stephen, a man full of faith and the Holy Spirit, and Philip, Prochorus, Nicanor, Timon, Parmenas, and Nicolas, a proselyte from Antioch, whom they set before the apostles; and when they had prayed, they laid hands on them. (Acts 6:5-6) NKJV

The multitude was pleased with this plan. Seven men were chosen and set before the apostles. All seven men had Greek names, suggesting they were Hellenists. They would work together to ensure the business of caring for all the widows was done for the glory of God.

They named the seven men. Everyone knew who was responsible for this ministry. Each of these men had good reputations. Each of these men was full of the Holy Spirit. Each of these men was full of wisdom.

There was a limit to the number of men. Only seven were chosen. Some other men may have been considered. Some other men may or may not have been equally qualified. Some men may have been unwilling. Some men may have been unavailable. **However, these seven men were...**up for the assignment, ready for the challenge, prepared for the procedure, able for the duty, willing for the work, equipped for the effort, and motivated for the ministry.

These seven men were of honorable quality and filled with the Spirit of God. At least two of them, Stephen and Philip, became dynamic and effective preachers of the Gospel. When accused of blasphemy, Stephen boldly, methodically, historically, and truthfully proclaimed the Gospel. After the great lamentation made for Stephen, the Church was scattered. Philip went down to Samaria preaching Christ.

"Then the word of God spread, and the number of the disciples multiplied greatly in Jerusalem, and a great many of the priests were obedient to the faith." (Acts 6:7)

After they met this challenge, the word of God spread. The number of the disciples multiplied greatly in Jerusalem. After they chose, prayed, and laid hands on these seven men, the church multiplied.

They met this challenge because the twelve never lost sight of the big picture. The twelve always kept the mission in their minds. The twelve remembered the Great Commission! They remembered the words of Jesus, "But you shall receive power when the Holy Spirit has come upon you; and you shall be witnesses to Me in Jerusalem, and in all Judea and Samaria, and to the end of the earth" (Acts 1:8)!

By choosing others to deal with the challenge of the complaint, the way was cleared for "a great many of the priests to be obedient to the faith" (Acts 1:7).

This is a significant statement. The priests were the teachers of the Law. They officiated at the temple worship and sacrifices, and made their living performing religious functions. A great many priests were willing to leave and abandon their posts knowing it would change their lifestyles. In addition, if the priests were leaving the Old Law, then there would ultimately be an end to blood sacrifices. This would end because the sacrifice of Christ put an end to all animal sacrifice (Hebrews 10:1-18).

Discussion Questions

1. In what ways can men be problem solvers?
2. What qualities did the people look for in the men?
3. What are the qualities women value in men?
4. Why does the church thrive when men are empowered to work together?
5. Why is it important for a man to be full of the Holy Spirit?
6. Why are men important to the growth of the church?

Chapter 8

MEN ARE NOT ALL THE SAME

1 Timothy 3:1-13

This is a faithful saying: If a man desires the position of a bishop, he desires a good work. A bishop then must be blameless, the husband of one wife, temperate, sober-minded, of good behavior, hospitable, able to teach; not given to wine, not violent, not greedy for money, but gentle, not quarrelsome, not covetous; one who rules his own house well, having his children in submission with all reverence (for if a man does not know how to rule his own house, how will he take care of the church of God?); not a novice, lest being puffed up with pride he fall into the same condemnation as the devil. Moreover he must have a good testimony among those who are outside, lest he fall into reproach and the snare of the devil. Likewise deacons must be reverent, not double-tongued, not given to much wine, not greedy for money, holding the mystery of the faith with a pure conscience. But let these also first be tested; then let them serve as deacons, being found blameless. Likewise, their wives must be reverent, not slanderers, temperate, faithful in all things. Let deacons be the husbands of one wife, ruling their children and their own houses well. For those who have served well as deacons obtain for themselves a good standing and great boldness in the faith which is in Christ Jesus. NKJV

There are various reasons for the painful absence of men from American households. This vital void in some cases has been caused by the untimely and unexpected death of a father and husband. In other instances, the man's absence from the household has been caused by the ugliness of divorce. Still another cause is the growing trend of single-mother households and unwed parents. Finally, in some situations, dad is absent due temporary circumstances such as military deployment, job placement, or incarceration.

This is not merely a quantitative question. There is sufficient concern about the growing absence of the male presence in the American household. This is also a qualitative question. In many households, a male is present, but only in the biological sense. When I ask, "Is there a man in the house," I am asking if there is a certain quality of man in the house? Is there a spirit-led man in the house? Is there a servant-leader man in the house? Is there a man of faith in the house? Is there a worshipping and praying man in the house? Is there a holy man in the house? Is there a dedicated man in the house?

The household is blessed by the presence of a Christ-centered man. Abraham's household was blessed by his presence. Isaac's household was blessed by his presence. Jacob's household was blessed by his presence.

Blessed is every one who fears the LORD, who walks in His ways. When you eat the labor of your hands, you shall be happy, and it shall be well with you. Your wife shall be like a fruitful vine in the very heart of your house,
Your children like olive plants all around your table.
Behold, thus shall the man be blessed who fears the LORD.

The LORD bless you out of Zion, and may you see the good of Jerusalem all the days of your life. Yes, may you see your children's children.
Peace be upon Israel! (Ps. 128:1-6)

How can modern man measure his manhood? There is an ancient standard, an old path. The profile of a Christ-centered man is found, oddly enough, in 1Timothy 3:1-13. Generally, this passage lists or defines the qualifications or qualities for bishops and deacons. Not all men are husbands and fathers; however, there is more to being a man than having a wife and children. This passage offers much in the way of understanding manhood because it describes essential spiritual qualities for every man. Outside of being a husband and father, every man should seek to excel in these qualities. However, this is also for every man with a wife and children because this profile should become his goal wherever possible.

It would be wise to issue a disclaimer here. This lesson is not intended to suggest only men appointed to be shepherds and deacons are real men. A man can meet the qualifications, yet not desire to be an overseer or deacon. However, this message is intended to teach important aspects of manhood and challenge all men to strive in their efforts to be Christ-centered men.

His Masculine Requisite

There are at least twelve uses of the masculine in this passage. This is indicative of the clear leadership responsibilities of men in both the church and the family. God has placed leadership responsibilities on their shoulders.

The male gender is a prerequisite for these positions of leadership, but it is far from being the only requirement. True leadership privileges are gained through permission and performance.

The leader must have God's permission to lead. The leader must also have the followers' permission and cooperation to lead. For instance, the wife is not to usurp his authority and the children are not to be insubordinate. The leader must demonstrate the ability and willingness to perform the duties of leadership.

Leadership is service oriented. At the heart of leadership is a loving concern to motivate, support, serve, teach, and guide people to become their very best for the glory of God. Leadership is about positively influencing followers to accept God's purpose and plan for their lives.

Let us offer a word of caution to the husbands and fathers. Edwin H. Friedman said, "People choose leaders because they promise to lead them to a happier or more fruitful state, but after the election, the followers invariably function either individually or in concert to frustrate their leaders' effect" (Friedman, p. 224). Eve did it to Adam. Solomon's wives did it to him. Absalom did it to David. Israel repeatedly did it to Moses. The disciples did it to Jesus!

Again, read this definition of biblical manhood: "At the heart of mature masculinity is a sense of benevolent responsibility to lead, provide for, and protect women in ways appropriate to a man's differing relationships" (Piper, p. 36).

His Mature Resume

Is there a mature man in the house? The apostle provides a partial list of the qualities possessed by a spiritually mature man. These qualities are essential to fulfilling his purpose. His role and responsibilities demand the acquisition and application of these qualities.

Time will not permit us to discuss these qualities exhaustively. These spiritual qualities enable men to lead and serve successfully.

These qualities are not only needed to lead in the church, but also to lead in the family and in every sector of society.

A mature man is blameless; there are no sustainable evil reports circulating against him. He guards his character and his past is put away. A mature man masters temperance and has the ability to self-govern and restrain himself from over-indulgence. He is sober in his thinking, a clear and balanced thinker, and committed to good behavior, especially toward others. He embraces the importance of hospitality toward others, especially strangers. He is able to teach because he has a sound and firm knowledge of the word of God.

A mature man is not given to drink, does not allow himself to be influenced or controlled by wine or other foreign substances. He is a not violent man. He is not greedy for money and does not acquire it by dishonorable means. He is gentle and forbearing even when encountering "trouble makers." A mature man is neither quarrelsome nor covetous.

His Managerial Relationships

The key word in this passage is "rule." It is the original term *proistemi*, which means to be at the head of, rule, and care for. The root word describes to lead, to direct, to assist, to protect, and to represent.[7]

The man is in the house for the purpose of caring for, leading, directing, and protecting his family. God has made him the head of the family. As a husband, he is a one-woman man. As a father, his children and household are under his guidance.

The man must have a spirit filled with the kind of character his family willingly admires and honors. The husband/father provides a vision for the family of the purpose and plan of God and keeps them on the course set by the Lord.

Discussion Questions

1. What does it mean for a man to rule his house?
2. How can a man's family demonstrate support for his leadership in the home?
3. Give some illustrations from fact or fiction (such as movies) in which a man felt the pressure of responsibility? How did it impact him? How did he cope with it?
4. What are some of the lessons you have learned from significant men in your life?

Chapter 9

MEN NEED TO FEEL RESPECTED

Men need respect—women need love. (Eph. 5:31-33)

A man needs to be king of his castle. The best way, really the only way, for a woman to be a queen is for her to make her husband the king. It is possible for both men and women to mutually satisfy the needs of one another. While the woman needs to be loved and the man's top priority, he also needs her to respect him. A man needs to know his wife has confidence in his ability to lead the family, make wise decisions and follow through on his word.

Please understand that we need to be respected, valued, appreciated by the people for whom we care: wives, children, and churches.

This need is a part of our biological make up that comes directly from God.

Men need and want reverence much like God; we are made in His image and likeness.

It feeds our egos.

It fuels our energies.

It formats our education.

It allows our heads to be held high.

It allows our chests to expand.

When a man is respected and when you are proud of him and share it, he will break his neck to live up to what have you said about him. Respect provides a man with a sense of validation and courage. When a man receives respect it builds his self-esteem and self-confidence.

Most men are aware of their imperfections and reminding them of their weaknesses usually does not motivate them to become better. It is more beneficial to look for the positive characteristics and actions taken by a man and commend him. This will inspire him more than berating him.

Discussion Questions

1. In what ways do you demonstrate respect for the men in your life?
2. Why is feeling respect so important to me?
3. Describe a time when you witnessed a man experience disrespect.
4. Why does an African-American man need respect at home?

Chapter 10

MEN EXPERIENCE HIGH LEVELS OF STRESS

1 Samuel 10:21-24

"When he had caused the tribe of Benjamin to come near by their families, the family of Matri was chosen. And Saul the son of Kish was chosen. But when they sought him, he could not be found. Therefore they inquired of the LORD further, "Has the man come here yet?" And the LORD answered, "There he is, hidden among the equipment." So they ran and brought him from there; and when he stood among the people, he was taller than any of the people from his shoulders upward. And Samuel said to all the people, "Do you see him whom the LORD has chosen, that there is no one like him among all the people?" So all the people shouted and said, "Long live the king!" NKJV

The story of Saul, Israel's first anointed king, serves as the background for our current dilemma. When God's people were assembled at Mizpah to witness the anointing and ordination of its anointed king, a puzzling picture appeared. The passage reads, "But when they sought him, he could not be found." (1 Sam. 10:21) The people faced a brief dilemma. They were seeking a man. They were looking for a king. They were anticipating a leader. They were hoping for a soldier and a warrior. "But when they sought him, he could not be found." (1 Sam. 10:21)

This is our current dilemma. It is a serious dilemma. We are looking for men. We are looking for godly men. We are looking for men "who walk not in the counsel of the ungodly nor stand in the path of sinners, nor sit in the seat of the scornful" (Psalm 1:1a). We are looking for good men. David said, "The steps of a good man are ordered by the Lord, and He delights in his way" (Ps. 37:23). We are desperately looking for men. We are looking for strong men, men with honor, courage, and integrity, real men. Our children are looking for men to be their fathers, women for men to become their husbands. The Church is looking for spirit-filled and spirit-led men to serve and lead in the church. Yes, we are looking for men. We are looking for men who are willing to stand up and be counted, willing to take responsibility for their actions, willing to face challenges and endure difficulties and face and fight the Goliaths of our day.

However, let us remind you of the dilemma. We are seeking them, yet they cannot be found. They are hidden from us and among us. We need them. We need their masculinity and strength, their intelligence and wisdom. We need their experience and their protection. We need men will to make provision for their families. We need their leadership, their discipline, and their creativity. Yet they are veiled from us. We cannot see them with our natural eyes because they are hidden among us. They are present, but we must ask God to reveal them. The people turned to the Lord when they could not find Saul. The passage reads, "Therefore they inquired of the Lord further Has the man come here yet? And the Lord answered there he is hidden among the equipment" (1 Sam. 10:22). It is interesting that the KJV of this passage translates baggage rather than equipment. Saul was right under their noses, but they couldn't find him until the Lord unveiled him.

There are men hidden among us. They do not attend services every Sunday, but they are among us. They do not participate in the service, but they are among us. They will not get involved in the ministry, but they are among us. They are not a part of any ministry, but they are among us. They are good men. They are hard-working men. Some are family men, but they are hidden among us. Their God-given potential and power is hidden underneath the equipment and baggage. This equipment or baggage in which Saul was hiding has a military context. He was hiding among the very supplies the people wanted him to use. Saul was supposed to use these supplies as his tools to fight for and defend the people. There are men hiding among their God-given tools. They are hiding among their jobs, their hobbies, their positions and possessions. There are also good men hiding among their past mistakes and failures.

They do not want to be discovered. They would rather play "hide and seek." They do not want to reveal their power and potential. Why was Saul hiding among the equipment? I believe this was for two reasons. First, he didn't have any self-confidence. Outwardly, Saul was impressive. Listen to the description of his physical appearance in 1 Samuel 9:2: "And he had a choice and handsome son whose name was Saul. There was not a more handsome person than he among the children of Israel. From his shoulders upward he was taller than any of the people." Like many men, Saul had an internal problem. He didn't think much of himself. He was a very doubtful and pessimistic man, the kind of man that gave up easily. When the "going got rough, he got going." For instance, when he was looking for his father's lost donkeys, he wanted to give up and return home. The servant with him had to offer him a solution to each of his objections. Again, when Samuel informed him of God's decision to make him King, Saul responded in doubt and dismay. "And Saul answered and said 'am I not a Benjamite, of the smallest of the tribes of Israel, and my family the least of all the families of the tribe of Benjamin? Why then do you speak like this to me" (1 Sam 9:21). Saul believed his self-worth depended on his family heritage.

However, from this passage we learn something very important. You do not need a royal pedigree for God to use you. Saul came from the lowest of the low. God often chose the most unlikely to be his special servants. God chose Moses, a man slow of speech. God chose Matthew, a tax collector. The disciples were described as ignorant and unlearned men. Some men are hiding because they do not think God can use them. They do not see the power and potential within them. God can use men from all backgrounds. It's never an issue of where or how you grew up. God can use men from the ghettos, slums, and housing projects. God can use men who grew up without fathers. It's not an issue of whether or not you graduated high school or received a GED, whether you went to trade school or Harvard. It's not an issue of how much money you make, or what kind of car you drive, or of what your father or grandfather did or didn't do. The true measure of a man is not on the outside. The true measure of a man is on the inside. It's not an issue of whether or not you have done things that you are ashamed of, as all of us fall into that category!

Second, Saul was hiding because he didn't have a good relationship with the Lord. This was obvious for many reasons. On several occasions, Saul didn't act according to God's will. He made an unlawful sacrifice. He made a foolish oath because he was consumed with the desire for revenge against his enemies. He spared King Agag when God said to kill him. He sent the young man David out to fight Goliath, then became enraged with jealousy and bent on destroying David when the people praised him. Saul lost his mind, the kingdom, and his life because he would not live by faith in the Lord. Saul was afraid to trust the Lord. He made the mistake of depending on himself for victory.

There are men hiding among us because they will not trust God. They do not have confidence in God's power to strengthen them beyond their capabilities. Initially, Saul did not want to become king because he was not depending on God. He forgot that God is the King of Kings! Men, God will equip you with the supernatural powers to do what you could not do otherwise. We do not depend on our own strength, courage, intelligence, endurance, and wisdom. We must depend on the Lord God. The Lord will give you the power to overcome your past, the courage to face your enemies. The Lord will give you the wisdom to deal with your problems and the heart to love your family. He will give you the confidence and conviction to serve Him and His people. When a man loves God, he will serve God. Jesus said if they loved Him, they should feed His sheep. (John 21:17)

Every man has a responsibility not only to his job, family, and society, he also has a responsibility to God and His Church. Every man has something to give and offer the church. No we do not have enough active men. As found in Ephesians 4:16: "From whom the whole body, joined and knit together by what every joint supplies, according to the effective working by which every part does its share, causes growth of the body for the edifying of itself in love." God never intended for men to just sit in his service. He expects men to act. This is not a worship society. Every man is equally important. As found in 1 Corinthians 12:14-15: "For in fact the body is not one member but many. If the foot should say, "Because I am not a hand, I am not of the body," is it therefore not of the body?"

There appears to be a deliberate attempt to destroy men. I believe Satan is after men because the destruction of men weakens the society, the home, and the church. The graves are filled with men of great potential who died prematurely because of senseless actions. The prisons are overflowing with men who have great potential and power. In their desires, men are turning away from women in favor of other men. Some older men are seducing young boys. Men with great potential and power are standing on the street corners and living off women. Women outnumber men on college campuses and in the church.

The enemy is using many weapons inside and outside to destroy men. The feminist movement is perhaps the greatest danger to manhood. It means something to be a man. There is something distinct and unique about masculinity. God intended for there to be a difference between men and women. However, the feminist movement has marred that distinction through the insistence that women be treated like men. Even in the early stages of development, there is a distinction between boy children and girl children. They play differently and generally choose different play toys. However, the feminist movement is the cause of many ungodly things. It has displaced the man's authority in the home to the point where he no longer has any authority. His position of leadership in the church is threatened. Our culture seems to be working against men. It rewards men for not taking responsibility. The welfare system will provide for a woman and her children, thereby absolving the man of his responsibility as provider. There are also a large number of women raising boys by themselves. This is not to say that women can't raise boys to become men, but it is much more difficult for them to do so without a godly man.

Perhaps we should describe and define a man. A man is strong, valiant, intelligent, and spiritual. He is powerful and mighty, a defender, protector, and a source of security. He is a son, a father, an uncle, a husband, a brother, a nephew, and a grandfather. He is a way maker and a pathfinder, a discoverer and an adventurer. He is a warrior, a hunter, a builder, and a fisherman. He is not ashamed of his masculinity and celebrates his manhood. He gives and demands respect. He likes to be in charge and is not afraid of being on the front lines. He disciplines, trains, and nurtures his children and loves his wife as he does himself. He opens his mouth in wisdom but will also admit his mistakes. He knows how to lead, but he is also willing to follow. He finds accomplishment through conquering. He needs recreation because he understands all work and no play is not good; at the same time, he needs competition because it drives him to become a better man. He speaks through his actions. He is the head of the woman, if he accepts Christ as his head (1 Cor. 11:3) and he serves as a priest in the home (Eph. 5:25-27).

The issue of manhood is compounded because we do not have an official rite of passage for men. There is no clear line between boyhood and manhood. Manhood is not determined by height and weight, by body or facial hair. Manhood is an honored state of masculinity. Manhood is not determined by the ability to reproduce or by sexual encounters. Manhood is not determined by fraternal order or gang membership. Manhood is indicated by survival. A man uses his God-given gifts and talents to survive. He is able to make the right decisions. He is willing to learn from his mistakes.

We are convinced there are extremely powerful men among us, but they are hiding among the baggage. We need to inquire of the Lord so that He can reveal them. We are convinced there are some strong, valiant, intelligent men at this church. Men who need to put their faith in the Lord and stand up and be counted. Men who have much to contribute and could really be a blessing to this ministry. There are men here on the verge of greatness, much like Saul was. God wants to use you in His service. God is looking for a few good men, men of faith, men filled with the Holy Spirit. The world needs men willing to declare their personal faith in the ability of God to do anything but fail.

The Psalmist said, "When I consider Your heavens, the work of your fingers, the moon and the stars, which You have ordained, what is man that You are mindful of him, and the son of man that You visit him? For You have made him a little lower than the angels, and You have crowned him with glory and honor." (Ps.

8:3-5) God has marked man with distinction so as to remember him. God has given special consideration to man. He has clothed man with both glory and honor. We are made just a little lower than the angels. We are the highest of God's earthly creation. Again the Psalmist speaks and as men we need to listen:

> For You formed my inward parts; You covered me in my mother's womb. I will praise You, for I am fearfully and wonderfully made; Marvelous are Your works, and that my soul knows very well. My frame was not hidden from You, when I was made in secret, and skillfully wrought in the lowest parts of the earth. Your eyes saw my substance, being unformed. And in Your book they were all written, the days fashioned for me, when as yet there were none of them. (Ps 139:13-16).

No man is a mistake. God has made us strong. He has built within us this maleness. He has equipped us with everything we need to be men.

It's time for our men to stand on the battlefield.

We can no longer sit on the sidelines because "For God has not given us the spirit of fear, but of power and of love and of a sound mind." (2 Tim 1:7)

We are God's army: "You therefore must endure hardship as a good soldier of Jesus Christ. No one engaged in warfare entangles himself with the affairs of this life that he may please him who enlisted him as a soldier." (2 Tim 2:3-4)

Ladies You Can Still Find Some Good Godly Men With God's Help

When He needed an ark builder, He found Noah.
When He needed a man to build a nation, He found Abraham.

58

When He needed a man to stand before Pharaoh, He found Moses.
When He needed a man to take them into the promised land, He found Joshua.
When He needed a man to fight Goliath, He found David.
When He needed a man of wisdom, He found Solomon.
When He needed a man of strength, He found Samson.
When He needed a man of integrity, He found Job.
When He needed a man of prayer, He found Daniel.
When He needed a man to rebuild the wall, He found Nehemiah.
When He needed a man to stand against the prophets of Baal, He found Elijah.
When He needed a man to preach in Nineveh, He found Jonah.
When He needed a man to preach to dry bones, He found Ezekiel.

Discussion Questions

1. What are some of the causes of male stress?
2. What can you do to help lessen men's levels of stress?
3. What does stress do to the mind, body, and spirit?
4. What are some maladaptive ways of dealing with stress?

Chapter 11

MEN NEED FRATERNITY TO SURVIVE

M en need fraternity. We need bonding/common interests with other men. The Church will expand and grow overnight when we see and address a man's need for fraternity.

Men need friendships, mutual connections, and feelings of brotherhood. We need this kinship. We need solidarity, union with our brothers.

The Church is often almost hostile to this idea. Jesus and the twelve disciples were really a fraternity. They slept together. They were in class together, learning at the feet of Jesus. Contrary to popular belief, the twelve followed a man that they respected. This was a man who called and chose them to be in a spiritual fraternity.

Men often join fraternities (Greeks) and they join gangs. Professional associations feed this desire to bond with other men.

Men are also fighting for survival.

The silent trends and norms of society have further emasculated men. All of the trends (though not necessarily bad) are in favor of women. The military now includes women, which further contributes to the diminished society of men. The military is infiltrated by women, as are Congress, the Senate, our court systems and judges, and heads of state. Women are the heads of families, heads of corporations, and CEOs of Fortune 500 companies.

Women have even commandeered the pulpits in many so-called churches.

Our school system and more have contributed to the emasculation of men in church and society. The persistent attack against men, whether intentional or unintentional, has helped lead to a crisis within the male species.

Discussion Questions

1. Why do men typically have so few friends?
2. How do male friendships differ from female friendships?
3. Discuss the friendship between Jonathan and David (1 Samuel 18).
4. Why are some young men attracted to gangs?
5. What is friendship?

Chapter 12

THE CALL TO FATHERING

Genesis 17

G enesis is the book of beginnings. It records the origins of humanity and describes societal development. It is the manual on Creation, on Elohim, the Triune God. It speaks everything into reality. There is no talk about a big bang or a mystic cosmic expansion. The three-in-one God stood on nowhere in time without end and created everywhere in time.

It is the beginning of anthropology, the beginning of language and civilization. It is the beginning of human relationships, of sciences, mathematics, and arts. Yes, in the beginning, God created the heavens and the earth.

It is also a book of genealogy. It begins with the creation of a man and a woman. Adam and Eve were fruitful and they multiplied. They reproduced not only their genes, but also their faith, traditions, experiences, hopes, dreams, and disappointments.

Genesis is also a book of blessing and cursing. In the beginning, God blessed His creation. He pronounced His delight with His creation and blessed humanity with the ability and resources to thrive by fulfilling their purpose. Man and Woman had His word. They had His presence. They had His provision.

However, given free will, they chose to step outside heaven's restrictions. As a result, they came to know good and evil. Imagine a state of existence absent the knowledge of evil. Contemplate a reality without an awareness of evil. Sin enters into the equation. Now there exists both blessings and curses.

The curiosity of desiring to know evil caused the collapse of humanity from the heights of heaven's sweetest blessings down to the lowest depths of bitter death. We were curious to know all of the awful ugliness of evil. **We were curious to know...**

The wastefulness of wickedness
The mischievousness of malevolence
The seductiveness of sin
The ominous intrigue of iniquity
The ingratiating allure of immorality
The villainous voices of vice
The despicable dogma of depravity
The disgraceful dramas of decadence
The creepy delights of corruption
The portentous pleasures of self-indulgence

Knowing evil changed everything, including the family. In Genesis, we are exposed to the starting point of family. God created family. Perhaps the Godhead wanted humanity to experience a similar warmth and oneness. Genesis describes the *first marriage*, the *first husband*, the *first wife*, the *first father*, the *first mother*, the *first children*, the *first siblings*, and the *first grandparents*.

Families of today can look back to Genesis to find hope and instruction for themselves. In Genesis, we find real families. Not only do we see the family as it was designed, but we also see the family flawed. Husbands and wives wavered in their roles. Cain killed his brother Abel. Lamech took not one but two wives. Reuben slept with his father's wife. Joseph's brothers sold him into slavery. Rachel and Leah competed for the same man. Abram fathered a child with Hagar. Jacob conned Esau out of his birthright and deceived his father for the blessing. Laban deceived Jacob on his wedding night. Lot's wife looked back and turned to a pillar of salt. Prince Shechem defiled Dinah. Simeon and Levi slaughtered the Hivites. Judah impregnated his daughter-in-law disguised as a harlot. Yes, these are real families with real issues!

Their family struggles and successes offer us hope. In many ways, our families are just as flawed. Husbands are abdicating their roles as family heads. Parents are failing to govern and train their children while children are rebelling against their parents. Siblings are growing apart. Yes, many of our families are in trouble.

Our families are in serious trouble because of irresponsible fathering. We have too many appeasing fathers and avenging sons (*the story of Dinah*). We have too many apathetic fathers and angry sons (*the story of Tamar*). The importance of the father and his role is being overlooked. The final verse of the Old Testament warns us of the devastating consequences of fatherlessness: "His preaching will turn the hearts of fathers to their children, and the hearts of children to their fathers. Otherwise I will come and strike the land with a curse" (Mal 4:6) NLT.

It is not only a cause for grave concern, but it is also a cursed condition when the hearts of fathers and their children are not turned toward one another. Too many fathers are dreadfully distant from their children. No wonder God is the helper of the fatherless (Ps 10:14). The Lord relieves the fatherless (Ps 146:9). He is merciful to the fatherless (Hos 14:3) because the Lord understands the consequences of being fatherless.

We now have a different degree of societal fatherlessness. We have a crisis of fatherlessness through denial and disposal.

He was there for the conception, but not for the caring.

He was there for the deposit, but not for the discipline.

He was there for the planting, but not for the provision of the children.

He was there for the making, but not for the maturing.
He was there for the sowing, but not for the reaping.
He was there for the pleasure, but not for the parenting.

Fathering is a Call to Responsibility

When Abram was ninety-nine years old, the LORD appeared to Abram and said to him, "I am Almighty God; walk before Me and be blameless. And I will make My covenant between Me and you, and *will multiply you exceedingly.*" Then Abram fell on his face, and God talked with him, saying: "As for Me, behold, My covenant is with you, and you shall be a father of many nations. No longer shall your name be called Abram, *but your name shall be Abraham; for I have made you a father of many nations. I will make you exceedingly fruitful; and I will make nations of you, and kings shall come from you.* And I will establish My covenant between Me and you and your *descendants* after you in their generations, for an everlasting covenant, *to be **God to you and your descendants** after you.* Also I give to you and your descendants after you the land in which you are a stranger, all the land of Canaan, as an everlasting possession; and *I will be their God.*" (Gen. 17:1-8) NKJV

We have raised a generation of men without models of biblical masculinity![8] But Abraham serves as a valid and valuable model for any man of faith. He is a superb model of fathering. Through Abraham, we learn that fathering is a call to responsibility.

The joy and happiness of fathering comes from being responsible. Joy can never be achieved through whining, belly-aching, and whimpering about the disasters and struggles of life. Joy is achieved through rigorous effort and responsible action. Joyous people are too busy to think about being unhappy. Thoreau said, "that man is the richest whose pleasures are the cheapest." Rudyard

Kipling said, "If you can meet with Triumph and Disaster/ and treat those two impostors just the same...you'll be a Man, my son!"

At the time of this passage, Abram was a ninety-nine-year old man. He had been waiting on God to fulfill His promise for fertility for nearly twenty-five years. When he was eighty-six years old, he and Sarai proceeded ahead of God and he fathered Ishmael with Hagar, the Egyptian handmaid.

In actuality, the Lord had already decreed this covenant in Genesis 15. Righteousness was accounted to Abram because He believed in the Lord (Gen. 15:6). The Lord solidified His promise to give the land of Canaan to Abram as an inheritance through the ratification of the covenant. In this instance, the Lord was guaranteeing His word to Abram.

The Lord instructed Abram to bring Him five animals: a three-year-old heifer, a three-year-old female goat, a three-year-old ram, a turtledove, and a young pigeon. Abram cut the animals in two with the exception of the turtledove and young pigeon. A deep sleep fell on Abram. While he was in this deep sleep, the Lord spoke to Abram and told him about his future. However, at the end of this deep sleep, the Lord appeared symbolized by a smoking oven and a burning torch. The smoking oven and burning torch passed through the animals. This was the common form of covenant making. The Lord obligated Himself to fulfill His promise to Abram concerning land.

Genesis 17 speaks to God's covenant with Abram regarding an heir and descendants. Fathering was a spiritual concept. The call to fathering was initiated by the instructions "I am Almighty God; walk before Me and be blameless." This was not only a call to responsibility, but a call to righteousness. Wholeness is obtained by walking before God; this means placing yourself under His exclusive supervision, guidance, and protection.[9]

The goal of the Lord is to be God to us. He seeks godly offspring (Mal. 2). Godly offspring are typically the product of godly people. Abram's fathering is based on the preexisting supposition that he walked blamelessly before God. The Lord wanted Abram to be under His Divine supervision prior to Abram having children under his supervision.

At some point we must see the connection between our relationship with God and our role as fathers. Notice that Genesis 17:2 begins with the conjunction "and." The Lord was making this covenant with Abram predicated on his blameless walking before Him. The Lord was cautious about what He multiplied.

The Lord wanted to multiply righteousness, faithfulness, obedience, and trust. The Lord had no desire to multiply unrighteousness, disbelief, or disobedience. The Lord knew that when He multiplied Abram, He would get more of what was in Abram.

Strive to be a father that multiplies awesome attributes and qualities. When the Lord multiplies you, He should be multiplying wisdom, faith, integrity, responsibility, goodness, justice, grace, mercy, diligence, strength, kindness, maturity, self-denial, confidence, courage, vision, hope, wealth, worship, prayer, service, humility, and love.

Fathering requires an acceptance of responsibility. A wise man uses divine truth to guide how he fathers his children. This is preferred to using past hurts and personal injuries along with other subjective feelings to guide the work of fathering.

This principle is seen in the Scriptures. In Genesis 17:5, the Lord says, "no longer shall your name be called Abram, but your name shall be Abraham; for I have made you a father of many nations." The name Abram means "exalted" with respect to a father. It signified that Abram was from a distinguished lineage and high or noble birth.[10] The name Abraham means "father of a multitude." Abraham was no longer to look back at his past.

He was now to look forward toward his future descendants. It can be difficult to father while still licking the wounds of your past. Your fathering can suffer as long as you suck on the nipple of self-pity. Your fathering is diminished as long as you belly-ache about all of the injustices, atrocities, traumas, obstacles, and hardships you have had to endure. Fathering is ineffective while you seek pampering, validation, affirmation, and self-gratification.

Fathering is a responsibility, a responsibility to God, to self, andto our sons and daughters. It is a responsibility to walk before God. It is a responsibility to finish what was started at the conception and to behave and function as a fully responsible adult.

It is a responsibility to love.

It is a responsibility to teach.

It is a responsibility to nurture.

It is a responsibility to discipline.

It is a responsibility to provide.

It is a responsibility to bring children up in the nurture and admonition of the Lord.

It is a responsibility to protect.

It is a responsibility to guide.

It is a responsibility to model.

It is a responsibility to stay up at night with a sick child.

It is a responsibility to change diapers and feed.

It is a responsibility to sacrifice.

It is a responsibility to do things you do not feel like doing.

It is a responsibility to comfort their fears.

It is a responsibility to encourage their success.

It is a responsibility to guide their choices.

It is a responsibility to take them on doctor and dental visits.

It is a responsibility to love them unconditionally.

Fathering is a Call to Ritual

> And God said to Abraham: "As for you, you shall keep My covenant, you and your descendants after you throughout their generations. This is My

68

covenant which you shall keep, between Me and you and your descendants after you: Every male child among you shall be circumcised; and you shall be circumcised in the flesh of your foreskins, and it shall be a sign of the covenant between Me and you. He who is eight days old among you shall be circumcised, every male child in your generations, he who is born in your house or bought with money from any foreigner who is not your descendant. He who is born in your house and he who is bought with your money must be circumcised, and My covenant shall be in your flesh for an everlasting covenant. And the uncircumcised male child, who is not circumcised in the flesh of his foreskin, that person shall be cut off from his people; he has broken My covenant." (Gen. 17:9-14) NKJV

Circumcision was the sign of God's covenant with Abraham. It was a perpetual ritual to be performed by Abraham and his descendants throughout their generations. Circumcision was the sign of the covenant because it was a promise for an innumerable multitude of descendants. Abraham was not the father of a nation, but many nations. He would be the progenitor of nations and kings would come from him. Abraham would be exceedingly fruitful.

It was a sign to both God and the people. Every male child would be circumcised in the flesh of his foreskin. This was done on the eighth day of life:

At birth, a baby has nutrients, antibodies, and other substances from his mother's blood, including her blood-clotting factors, one of them being prothrombin. Prothrombin is dependent on vitamin K for its production. Vitamin K is produced by

69

intestinal bacteria, which are not present in a new-born baby. After birth, prothrombin decreases so that by the third day it is only 30 percent of normal. Circumcision on the third day could result in a dev-astating hemorrhage.

The intestinal bacteria finally start their task of man-ufacturing vitamin K, and the prothrombin subse-quently begins to climb. On day eight, it actually overshoots to 110 percent of normal, leveling off to 100 percent on day nine and remaining there for the rest of a person's healthy life. Therefore, the eighth day was the safest of all days for circumcision to be performed. On that one day, a person's clotting factor is at 110 percent, the highest ever, and that is the day God prescribed for the surgical process of circumcision.

Today, vitamin K (Aqua-Mephyton) is routinely administered to newborns shortly after their delivery, and this eliminates the clotting problem. However, before the days of vitamin K injections, a 1953 pedi-atrics textbook recommended that the best day to circumcise a newborn was the eighth day of life.[11]

Glory to God! He wanted them to bleed, but He did not want them to bleed out. The Lord protects us in our pain. He gives us grace in our suffering. He shows us mercy in our misery. He tem-pers our trials. He prepares us before He tests us.

Everyone both born and bought was to be circumcised. The biological and non-biological were to be one in the covenant family! Circumcision also symbolized purity. *They were to be either cut on or cut off!*

The ritual of fathering is introducing and including your descendants in a covenant with God. Ultimately, this physical circumcision was understood in terms of circumcision of the heart (Deut. 30:6; Ps. 118:10; Rom. 2:28-29). Fathers should lead their children in rituals that promote the importance of living by faith in the Lord and in His promises. Such rituals can in include the practice of prayer and the study of Scripture.[12]

Fathering is a Call to Relationships

> Then God said to Abraham, "As for Sarai your wife, you shall not call her name Sarai, but Sarah shall be her name. And I will bless her and also give you a son by her; then I will bless her, and she shall be a mother of nations; kings of peoples shall be from her." Then Abraham fell on his face and laughed, and said in his heart, "Shall a child be born to a man who is one hundred years old? And shall Sarah, who is ninety years old, bear a child?"; And Abraham said to God, "Oh, that Ishmael might live before You!" Then God said: "No, Sarah your wife shall bear you a son, and you shall call his name Isaac; I will establish My covenant with him for an everlasting covenant, and with his descendants after him. And as for Ishmael, I have heard you. Behold, I have blessed him, and will make him fruitful, and will multiply him exceedingly. He shall beget twelve princes, and I will make him a great nation. But My covenant I will establish with Isaac, whom Sarah shall bear to you at this set time next year." Then He finished talking with him, and God went up from Abraham. (Gen. 17:15-22) NKJV

71

Abraham's fathering included a relationship with his wife Sarah. *Abraham was a husband before he became a father.* Sarah was Abraham's marital and parental partner. Her name was changed just as his name was changed. This barren wife would become the mother of nations and kings!

The best fathering occurs in the context of a healthy marital relationship. Abraham and Sarah had what Dr. Frank Pittman called "a grown-up marriage." Dr. Pittman said, "For the relationships to work out right, fathers must be just as involved as mothers in child raising from birth, and certainly from weaning." Pittman continued, "There is nothing in life that can make a man happier, more emotionally whole, or more adult than hands-on child raising. The man who avoids it is trying to guard his own childishness. He is a fool and unfortunately will remain a fool because he is skipping the experience that would give him grown-up wisdom."[13]

In the passage, Abraham grappled with and grounded his faith. He was overwhelmed with the supernatural power required to bring about such a reality. He was almost one hundred years old. Sarah was practically ninety years old and barren.

When confronted with the facts of his situation and the promise of God, Abraham exclaimed *"Oh, that Ishmael might live before You!"* Ishmael was Abraham's thirteen-year old son by Hagar. However, Ishmael was not the son conceived of faith. Ishmael was not the son of this promise. Most fathers want their "Ishmaels" to live before God!

One of the painful parts of fathering is accepting that God has different plans for all of your children. God blessed Ishmael because he was Abraham's son, but he was not the promised heir. Ishmael didn't do too badly. The Lord blessed Ishmael, made him fruitful, and multiplied him. Ishmael was the progenitor of twelve princes and became a great nation. *Fathering requires having a loving relationship with all of your children, regardless of God's plan for them.*

Discussion Questions

1. What are a father's responsibilities?
2. What does fathering look like when the children do not live in the same home as the father?
3. How can a father build healthy relationships with his children?
4. What do you think about Frank Pittman's comments about the need for fathers to be just as involved with their children from birth as their mothers?
5. What was the spiritual significance of circumcision?

Chapter 13

THINGS MEN WANT WOMEN TO KNOW

A group of Christian men were willing to unveil their vulnerabilities and share things they wanted their families to know about men. There is not enough room to discuss or list them all in this chapter. However, the following statements reveal much about the hidden hurts and hearts of men:

"Sometimes I do not know what I am doing."

"I just want your affection and to be understood."

"It's hard for me to balance everything without your help."

"It's hard for me to express my feelings."

"I try to put God first and I want my family to do the same."

"Respect me."

"I need to accomplish things."

"Money doesn't grow on trees; you have to work for it."

"Making decisions is not easy."

"I need a support system."

"I'm hard on you because I want you to be the best you can be."

"I want to explain what's happened in my past to explain why I am the way I am."

"I want to be a leader in my house, but sometimes my wife won't let me."

"It's important for me to feel wanted and needed."

"I fear failure."

"I do not know how to effectively express how I feel."

"I feel like I am always under a microscope."

"It is a struggle to keep yourself set apart and not fall victim to your vices."

"I love you (family) regardless."

Discussion Questions

1. Which statement speaks to you the most and why?
2. Which statement is most surprising to you?
3. Why is it hard for men to express their feelings?
4. What can you do to make life better for your husband or father?

Chapter 14

MEN AND WOMEN ARE DIFFERENT

The Role of Men and Women in Creation

The record of biblical creation is found in Genesis 1 and 2. God created humanity, both male and female, in His image (Gen 1:26-28). Humanity created in the image of God is significant.[14] The created is a reflection of the Creator. There are various explanations for the meaning of a humanity created in the image of God. Allen P Ross, in explaining "image" wrote, "The term must therefore figuratively describe human life as a reflection of God's spiritual nature, that is, human life has the communicated attributes that came with the inbreathing (Gen 2:7)."[15] Michael F. Stitzinger explained the image with regard to the ontological or spiritual attributes when he wrote, "The image of God is usually understood to include the will or freedom of choice, self-consciousness, self-transcendence, self-determination, rationality, moral discernment for good and evil, righteousness, holiness, and worship."[16]

Furthermore, Bruce A. Ware explained and evaluated three traditional views of image that he labeled as follows: structural, relational, and functional.[17] Although all three views hold merit, we found greater value in the functional view as it relates to this study. Ware wrote:

The image of God in man as functional holism
means that God made human beings, both male
and female, to be created and finite representations
(images of God) of God's own nature, that in relationship with him and each other, they might be his
representatives (imaging God) in carrying out the
responsibilities he has given to them. In this sense,
we are images of God in order to image God and
his purposes in the ordering of our lives and carrying out of our God-given responsibilities.[18]

The structure, relationship, and function of male and female
is necessary to understanding the roles of men and women in the
family, church, and society. In essence, it is a search to understand
what it means to be human. Understanding Deity aids in discov-
ering humanity. As Ware stated, males and females are "representations of God's own nature." A.W. Tozer (1897–1963), in his
classic work, *The Knowledge of the Holy*, described the importance of thinking properly about God when he wrote:

Among the sins to which the human heart is prone,
hardly any other is more hateful to God than idolatry, for idolatry is at bottom a libel on His character. The idolatrous heart assumes that God is
other than He is – in itself a monstrous sin – and
substitutes for the true God one made after its own
likeness. Always this God will conform to the
image of the one who created it and will be base
or pure, cruel or kind, according to the moral state
of the mind from which it emerges.[19]

In the above statement, Tozer described the human tendency to conform the Creator to the created rather than allow the Creator to inform the mind and transform the heart of His creation.

The creation account of Genesis 1–2 informs humanity on several important ideas. The first important idea of the creation account is God. Nothing happens in history until God acts. Belief in the existence of God remains a matter of faith (Heb. 11:1, 3, 6). The creation account presents a singular yet plural God. In Genesis 1:26, the plural is used in the phrases "let us," "in our image," and "our likeness." Ross admitted the plural in this verse is a source of debate among theologians.[20] Ross also saw harmony between these verbs and the plural form of God (Elohim) in Genesis 1:1; in addition, he asserted, the plurals permit the doctrinal development of the Trinity.[21] The Trinity is difficult to define,[22] but Kenneth Daughters favored a definition offered by James R. White: "Within the one Being that is God, there exists [sic] eternally three coequal and coeternal Persons, namely the Father, the Son, and the Holy Spirit."[23]

An understanding of the Trinity informs us here because God created males and females in His image and likeness. The above definition describes the Trinity or Godhead as coequal. The Father, the Son, and the Holy Spirit are equal in Deity. They share the divine essence. None of them is superior or inferior to the others. Millard Erickson (Professor, Theology, Baylor University) included the affirmation of deity as qualitatively the same in the Father, Son, and Holy Spirit.[24]

Similarly, male and female are equal in essence, worth, and value. Ware wrote: "Complementarians and egalitarians have agreed that the creation of male and female as the image of God indicates the equal value of women with men as being fully human, with equal dignity, worth, and importance."[25] This is an important affirmation because the battle over male and female gender relates to the issue of equality. Betty Friedan, a leader in the Feminist

Movement, wrote the following reflections on the twentieth anniversary of her now classic work, *The Feminine Mystique*:

> It was only after we broke through the feminine mystique and said women are people, no more no less, and therefore demanded our human right to participate in the mainstream of society, to equal opportunity to earn and be trained and have our own voice in the big decisions of our destiny, that the problems of women themselves became visible, and women began to take their own experience seriously.[26]

As previously stated, the roles of men and women in the family, church, and society involves anthropology. The proponents for feminism are dissatisfied partly because women have historically felt less than human due to inequality and discrimination in the home, workplace, politics, and education.[27]

The creation account of Genesis 1–2 affirms the equality of both male and female. Wayne Grudem (Research Professor, Bible and Theology, Phoenix Seminary) wrote:

> But if we are equally in God's image, then certainly men and women are equally important to God and equally valuable to him. We have equal worth before him for all eternity. The fact that both men and women are said by Scripture to be "in the image of God" should exclude all feelings of pride or inferiority and any idea that one sex is "better" or "worse" than the other. In particular, in contrast to many non-Christian cultures and religions, no one should feel proud or superior because he is a

man, and no one should feel disappointed or inferior because she is a woman.[28]

However, the creation account also affirms differences between
male and female equals. First, there are differences within the roles
of the Trinity.[29] The Father, Son, and Holy Spirit assume different
roles in creation and redemption.[30] The Father initiates the work
of creation through the Son and the Spirit sustains creation.[31] The
Son submits and subordinates Himself to the Father in redemption
(Luke 22:42; John 16:7; Phil. 2:6-8); however, this does not make
the Son inferior to the Father.[32] In describing the order of relations
within the Trinity, Robert Letham concluded there is authority and
obedience because the Father sends the Son and the Son obeys.[33]

Second, there are differences in the roles of males and females
as expressed in the creation account (Gen. 2:15-25). God creates
the man as leader and the woman as helper. David Lee Talley,
(Professor, Theology, Biola University) claimed the aforemen-
tioned as a teaching implication of Genesis 2 as follows:

> In the world which God created with all of the
> goodness in it, it is not good for the man, who func-
> tions as ruler in the garden, to be alone. So God
> creates a woman out of his rib. As such, the woman
> is uniquely given the responsibility to complete
> the man as his "corresponding opposite," being a
> "helper suitable" to him, so he will not be alone
> in fulfilling his tasks of ruling and subduing. The
> issue is not one of having another "leader" in the
> garden but, rather, one of companionship and com-
> pleting the man. God gives the man the woman to
> be his helper in carrying out his tasks.[34]

Furthermore, Stitzinger described eight signs of the man's leadership or headship based on the readings of Genesis 1–3.[35] The most compelling of these signs is basic. God creates man first. Before God creates the woman, God gives the man a set of responsibilities and instructions concerning man's work and God's word. The man's work is to take care of the garden. God's word instructs the man not to eat from the forbidden tree. The man, therefore, must be responsible to teach and lead the woman in the work and in the word. Grudem explained it this way:

> The fact that God first created Adam, then after a period of time created Eve (Gen. 2:7, 18-23), suggests that God saw Adam as having a leadership role in his family. No such two-stage procedure is mentioned for any of the animals God made, but here it seems to have a special purpose. The creation of Adam first is consistent with the Old Testament pattern of "primogeniture," the idea that the firstborn in any generation in a human family has leadership in the family for that generation ....The fact that we are correct in seeing a purpose of God in creating Adam first, and that this purpose reflects an abiding distinction in the roles God has given to men and women, is supported by 1 Timothy 2:13, where Paul uses the fact that "Adam was formed first, then Eve" as a reason for restricting some distinct governing and teaching roles in the church to men.[36]

Egalitarians and complementarians agree the woman is created as a helper (Gen 2:18). However, there is disagreement on the meaning of the woman as a helper. Stanley Grenz (Professor, Theology and Ethics) and Denise Muir Kjesbo, (Assistant Professor,

Christian Education) described the disagreement from the egalitarian point of view when they wrote: "Egalitarians not only dispute the complementarian claim that helper means 'subordinate,' but they also claim that the Hebrew designation clearly indicates the equality of the sexes."[37] However, these authors contradicted themselves by implying female superiority when they wrote:

> The narrative of Genesis 2 presents the woman as the one who saves the man from his loneliness. In so doing, she does indeed function in the story as the crown of creation .... As we noted earlier, the creation of woman "for man" or as his "helper" means that she rescues him from his solitude. Rather than being cast in a subservient role, she is thereby elevated in the narrative as the crowning achievement of God's saving intent for life in the Garden.[38]

In this case, the egalitarians are guilty of the same charges they level against the complementarians. As previously discussed, the role differences between men and women in the family, church, and society are solely functional. The differences in roles do not imply the superiority or inferiority of either gender.

The meaning of "helper" does not imply inferiority. The Hebrew term for helper (*ēzer*) means one who assists and serves another with what they need.[39] Mathews described the role of woman as helper when he writes:

> She is called Adam's "helper" (*ēzer*), which defines the role that the woman will play. In what way would Eve become a "helper" to the man? The term means "help" in the sense of aid and support and is used of the Lord's aiding his people in

the face of enemies (Pss 20:2, 3; 121:1-2; 124:8). Moses spoke of God as his "helper" who delivered him from Pharaoh (Exod. 18:4), and it is often associated with "shield" in describing God's protective care of his people.[40]

The Lord God was not diminishing the value or worth of the woman by assigning her the role of helper. God created woman as comparable or suitable to man for the purposes of aiding him in doing the work of God and fulfilling the word of God.

The Role of Men and Women and the Fall

The Fall of humanity, recorded in Genesis 3, is a defining point in history. In the Fall narrative, the serpent deceived the woman into eating from the forbidden tree and she gave the fruit to the man and he ate it. The Lord God punishes the serpent, the woman, and the man respectively for their involvement in the transgression. After the Fall, God banished the man and his wife from His presence (Gen. 3:23-24). Raymond C. Ortlund Jr. expressed the significance of the Fall when he wrote:

> Genesis 3 is one of the crucial chapters of Holy Scripture. If it were suddenly removed from the Bible, the Bible would no longer make sense. Life would no longer make sense. If we all started out in Edenic bliss, why is life so painful now? Genesis 3 explains why. And if something has gone terribly wrong, do we have any hope of restoration? Genesis 3 gives us hope.[41]

The Fall informs us because role violations contributed to the Fall, the Fall adversely affected the role relationship between men and women, and the primary role functions did not change after the Fall.

Though role violations contributed to the Fall, this is a point on which complementarians and egalitarians disagree. Grenz and Kjesbo expressed the differing views.

Complementarians claim that subordination is an order of creation. Egalitarians, in contrast, argue that it is a result of the Fall. Some complementarians, however, also appeal to the Fall, finding confirmation of male headship in the story of Genesis 3.[42]

This disagreement, of course, is a continuation of the oppositional views of creation as previously discussed. The egalitarians view the Fall as the origin of male domination. Grenz and Kjesbo wrote:

Egalitarians view the Fall in a very different light. They see God's intent in the creation narrative as one of male and female equality and complementarity, which precludes subordination. Genesis 3, in turn, recites the effects of sin on the original equitable relationship between the sexes.[43]

The authors add:

According to egalitarians, the narrator clearly intends for us to understand this statement as a reference to what resulted from sin, and not as a structure of creation. The narrator here gives us a general picture of the post-Fall state of affairs, not a command as to what either must be or should be. God declares that the advent of sin will bring changes in the relationship of the sexes.[44]

The narrator of Genesis 3 not only revealed the results of sin as Grenz and Kjesbo stated, the "narrator" described the causes of sin. The serpent deceived the woman, she ate, and the man followed his wife in eating from the tree.

The Lord God establishes the role of man as head and the woman as helper in creation, as previously noted. The fall into sin is clearly disobedience and breaking God's prohibitive law; on this point both complementarians and egalitarians agree. In creation, the man has a responsibility to keep God's word. As head, the man leads in the keeping of God's word and the implementation of God's work with woman as his helper. There are several indications that the violation of God's word included role violations on the part of both the woman and the man.

First, the serpent spoke to Eve concerning the word and will of God (Gen. 3:1-6). The serpent used his skillful craftiness to deceive the woman into eating the fruit. Grudem insightfully suggested the significance of the serpent approaching the woman first when he wrote:

> Satan, after he had sinned, was attempting to distort and undermine everything that God had planned and created as good. It is likely that Satan (in the form of a serpent), in approaching Eve first, was attempting to institute a role reversal by tempting Eve to take the leadership in disobeying God (Gen. 3:1). This stands in contrast to the way God approached them, for when God spoke to them, he spoke to Adam first (Gen. 2:15-17; 3:9). Paul seems to have this role reversal in mind when he says, "Adam was not deceived, but the woman

was deceived and became a transgressor." (1 Tim. 2:14) This at least suggests that Satan was trying to undermine the pattern of male leadership that God had established in the marriage by going first to the woman.[45]

The serpent challenged God's goodness. The woman believed the serpent's lie. The woman became dissatisfied with this one limitation. God gave them more than enough food by permitting them to eat freely from the trees of the Garden (Gen. 2:16). The woman ate because the serpent told her that she would become like God (Gen. 3:5). In the following writing, Betty Friedan also expressed this sense of dissatisfaction at the emergence of the women's liberation movement of the 1960s:

> The problem lay buried, unspoken, for many years in the minds of American women. It was a strange stirring, a sense of dissatisfaction, a yearning that women suffered in the middle of the twentieth century in the United States. Each suburban wife struggled with it alone. As she made the beds, shopped for groceries, matched slipcover material, ate peanut butter sandwiches with her children, chauffeured Cub Scouts and Brownies, lay beside her husband at night—she was afraid to ask even of herself the silent question: "Is this all?"[46]

Perhaps Eve was asking a similar question. She was in a perfect environment. God's presence was with her in the Garden. There was an abundance of food. There was no sin. She ruled, along with her husband, all of creation. Everything was good. They lived with God's blessing. Ironically, in a perfect environment, she experienced a sense of dissatisfaction.

Second, as a violation of her role, Eve usurped Adam's head-ship.[47] She gave him the fruit (Gen. 3:6). Instead of helping her husband keep God's word, she led him in disobeying God's law. David Lee Talley captured this idea when he wrote:

> The woman had been entrusted with the respon-sibility to follow the man (who was under the authority of the Creator). It was her duty to be the helpmeet to the man as he followed the Creator. When approached by the serpent, she abdicates (although deceived) her helping role by eating of the fruit, disregarding the word of the Creator given through the man (vertical relationship), and by acting independently, disregarding the leader-ship of the man (horizontal relationship).[48]

There is no indication from the passages of Genesis 3 that Eve's independent decision and consequent action is the result of abuse, neglect, or domination on the part of Adam. Eve did not make her decision because of oppression. Her defiance of God is an expression of her self-assumed position of headship over Adam.[49]

Third, Adam's involvement in the Fall is indicative of role violations. Eve did not act alone in sin. In fact, Adam bore pri-mary responsibility as the family head. Stitzinger described the situation as follows:

> The woman is often viewed as forcing, driving, or compelling her husband to eat. It is true that Adam participated in the sin because of his wife's offer (Gen. 3:6); however, he was not forced to eat the fruit. The account does not reveal whether Adam was present, passively listening to the serpent, or

if he was away at the time. V 17 declares that he "listened to" or "obeyed" the voice of his wife prior to eating the fruit, which may indicate that he was not there initially. In either circumstance, v 17 is the key; Adam freely chose to obey the voice of his wife. This sin actually began at the point when he failed to exercise his position of leadership over his wife. While Adam was not deceived, his action was equally as wicked as Eve's. Not until he sinned was the entire human race plunged into sin (Rom. 5:19; 1 Cor. 15:22). The sin of the first human beings was a direct violation of God's command, which expressed itself, in part, by a complete inversion of the roles. This was a total distortion of the pattern established in Genesis 1 and 2.[50]

The Lord God's response to their sin is further evidence of role violations as a major contributing factor in the Fall. Unlike the serpent, God spoke to Adam. Grudem wrote:

Just as God spoke to Adam on his own even before Eve was created (Gen. 2:15-17), so, after the Fall, even though Eve had sinned first, God came first to Adam and called him to account for his actions: "But the LORD God called to the man, and said to him, 'Where are you?' "(Gen. 3:9). God thought of Adam as the leader of his family, the one to be called into account first for what had happened in the family. It is significant that though this is after sin has occurred, it is before the statement to Eve, "He shall rule over you" in Genesis 3:16, where some writers today claim male headship in the family began.[51]

The Lord's punishment of Eve is evidence that He does not ignore her sin (Gen. 3:16). Although they are both responsible for their actions, Adam clearly has a greater sense of accountability.

Adam failed in his headship. He failed to lead his family in fulfillment of God's word and implementation of God's work.

Not only does the Fall reveal a violation of role responsibilities between the man and woman, but it also reveals the adverse effects of the Fall on the relationship between man and woman.[52] God punishes the woman's sin by making childbirth painful and giving her *desire* for her husband, who will *rule over* her (Gen. 3:16). We agree with Ortlund's conclusion that the woman's desire refers to her attempt to have her way with her husband and his ruling over her refers to the exercise of the man's godly headship.[53] Furthermore, the man's punishment was laborious toil in his work because he listened to his wife's voice rather than God's voice (Gen. 3:17-19). Similarly, Alexander Strauch, an author and elder for more than thirty years, described the adverse effects of the Fall as the distortion of the male and female relationship.[54]

The Fall adversely affected the role relationship between the man and the woman, but it did not initiate a new set of roles. The man and woman continued in the blessing of the Lord God because they were not cursed. The serpent and the ground were cursed (Gen. 3:14, 17). Humanity continued to live in their original assignment, albeit, in a fallen world filled with death, pain, sweat, and toil. The man continued as head of the relationship and the woman continued as his helper.

The Role of Men and Women in the Old Testament

The Old Testament does not bind Christians (Eph. 2:15; Col. 2:14; Heb 10:9; Rom. 7:6), but it is inspired Scripture (2 Tim. 3:15-17; 2 Pet. 1:20-21) and as Scripture, is good for both examples and learning in the life of faith (1 Cor. 10:1-13; Rom. 15:4). Therefore, the Old Testament informs us because it reveals the continuation of the roles of men and women established at creation. Although both men and women distort their roles at times, the Old Testament does not destroy the created roles. The man continues to be head or leader, under the authority of God, in order to guide his family in keeping God's word and doing God's work. Likewise, the woman continues as the man's helper in this created purpose. Furthermore, the Old Testament presents the roles of men and women in terms of family, the roles of men in patriarchy, and the life of women as helpers, some of which are exceptional.

We will follow the advice of John T. Willis (Professor, Old Testament, Abilene Christian University) who asserted the "absolutely imperative" decision to handle each statement about women within its own context while employing the best exegetical tools of individual capability.[55] Willis also provided three important guidelines for understanding the role of women in the Old Testament.[56] He wrote:

> First, the fact that an OT writer records an event or statement in which a man (or men) harbors a negative feeling toward a woman (or women) or treats a woman (women) in a negative way does not mean that the writer condones such a feeling or treatment or evidences a bias against women.[57]

> Second, the fact that an OT writer records an event or a statement in which a man (or men) exercises power over a woman (or women) does not mean that that writer approves of such activities, or that he/she is biased against women.[58]

> Third, the fact that an OT writer depicts woman in a subjective or dependent role does not mean that that writer either considers woman inferior to man or evidences a male chauvinistic attitude toward womankind.[59]

The Old Testament focuses on the family rather than the individual. God created family as the man and woman became one flesh (Gen. 2:18-25). The individuals of creation became one in purpose. This is important because individual interests generally characterize the difficulties between men and women concerning their roles. Joel F. Drinkard Jr. (Professor, Old Testament, Southern Baptist Theological Seminary) described this aspect of family life when he wrote:

> The "ideal" or "perfect" family existed no more in the Old Testament than today. In that sense the Old Testament doesn't try to present an overly idealized picture of families; it presents them "warts and all." The Old Testament is filled with examples of tensions, turmoil, and often tragedy surrounding, family life. Often the family members themselves are the chief causes of the tensions and turmoil, and ultimately the cause of much tragedy.[60]

The Old Testament vividly presents this realism. It is not that the individual ceases to exist in importance, but individuals come together in God's purpose. Whenever men or women choose to deviate from God's purpose, it adversely affects the family and not just the individual. Drinkard explained this concept as follows:

> The primary unit of society according to the Old Testament is the family. Quite in contrast to our western emphasis on individuality, Hebrew thought focused on group identity, specifically family identity. Saul, soon to be king over Israel, is not primarily the individual Saul; he is Saul, son of Kish (his father's household) of the Matrite Clan of the tribe of Benjamin (1 Sam. 9:1-2, 10:20-21). Likewise,

> Achan is identified as Achan, son of Carmi, son of Zabdi son of Zerah, of the tribe of Judah (Josh. 7:1). When he sins following the capture of Jericho, he brings disaster on all the people of Israel, not just himself. And his sin more specifically brings death and destruction to his entire household. As an aftermath to his sin, the people of Israel bring Achan, his sons and daughters, his oxen and donkeys and sheep, all in his household-even his tent-and burn and stone them all (Josh. 7:24-25).[61]

Throughout the Old Testament, the actions of both men and women positively or adversely affect the family based on their congruency with God's word and will. The decision of Lot's wife to disobey and look back left Lot a widower and their daughters consequently decided to get him drunk in order to have children (Gen. 19:26, 30-38). The wife of Moses, Zipporah, objected to circumcising her son and God sought to kill Moses because of it (Exod. 4:24-26). Jochebed's decision to keep her son alive rather than obey the Pharaoh's command to kill him led to the birth of Moses and deliverance of Israel (Exod. 2:1-10; 6:20). Esther's bold decision to risk death and go to the king without invitation led to the saving of Israel from annihilation (Esther 4:1-17). Esther's actions were consistent with her role as helper to her husband. Esther approached her husband with humility and used her influence to assist him in making a proper decision concerning God's people. Furthermore, the divorcing of wives by the men of Malachi's day adversely affected the families and not just the individual (Mal. 2:10-17).

Perhaps patriarchy best defines the role of men in the Old Testament. Although a majority of Christians believes in the patriarchal nature of the Old Testament, there are different conclusions about it.[62] Guenther Haas (Assistant Professor, Religion and Theology, Redeemer College) described five aspects of Old Testament patriarchy. Haas included the husband and father's role of leadership and the wife's childbearing and functional subordination to her husband. Furthermore, Haas asserted that the control of marriages was also patriarchal. Male elders, judges, prophets, and kings guided the civil affairs of the nation with a few exceptions. Religious life included both men and women, but men had unique requirements as family heads and functioned as priests.[63]

Although the Old Testament is patriarchal, women are significant, valuable, and worthy. Alexander Strauch described women's significance in the Old Testament as follows:

> Women are not missing from the Old Testament history of God's covenant people, however. Women prayed directly to God with great effectiveness, offered sacrifices to Him through the priests, and walked in intimate relationship with Him. Throughout the Old Testament, we read of many godly, heroic, influential women – women of amazing strength, wisdom, and competence. Although God makes His covenant with Abraham, for example, Sarah is a leading player in the story. Rebekah, Rachel, and Leah stand as prominent women alongside their patriarchal husbands. Although real love and devotion are demonstrated between these couples, there is also cruelty and manipulation.[64]

Strauch continued:

> The Old Testament doesn't paint a romantic or idealistic picture of the treatment of women. It paints a realistic portrait. The Old Testament shows the

cruelty of polygamy and the king's harem. We find examples of a double standard in sexual conduct (Gen. 38:11-26) under which men divorced their wives unjustly, but wives couldn't divorce their husbands.[65]

This realistic portrait of women in the Old Testament included a variety of situations. According to William E. Hull, (Research Professor, Samford University), women held a subordinate status in religious, legal, and domestic affairs in the time of the Old Testament.[66] Hull described the life of women in the patriarchy of the Old Testament:

> In the patriarchal system which lay at the foundation of Hebrew family life, a woman was subject to her father if single, to her husband if married, to her levir (husband's brother) or eldest son if widowed. In fact, the most typical Hebrew word for wife (ishshah) meant "woman belonging to a man," while one word for husband (baal) meant "owner of property." All of her rights were restricted by the dominion of the lord (adon) who ruled over her (Gen. 3:16b). He could repudiate her but she could not divorce him (Deut. 24:1-4). She had no rights of inheritance if there were male heirs (Num. 27:1-11). Even her religious vows unto the Lord could be nullified by father or husband if he disapproved (Num. 30:3-15).[67]

Although Hull's description may be disappointing, there is more to the story.[68] We agree with Willis that there are a number of Old Testament passages reflecting a high view of women.[69] Additionally, Julia P. Craig-Horne, (D.Min. Graduate) argued that a number of women experienced prominent roles in the Old Testament.[70] Willis described one of these high views from Proverbs 31:10-31 as follows:

> This text describes the "good wife" as priceless, faithful to her husband, industrious, generous, courageous, creative, strong, poised, kind, instructive, one who provides well for her household, praiseworthy, and one who fears God. There is no hint in this passage that she takes second place to her husband or anyone else. Indeed, because of her godly nature and character, her husband trusts in her and has no lack of gain (v.11), she does him good all the days of his life (v.12), and he is known in the gates (v. 23), i.e., he is respected as an outstanding, upright citizen of the community. But these observations do not reflect a male-dominated point of view. On the contrary, the woman described here is independent. On her own initiative, she develops a widespread mercantile business (vv. 13-14, 18, 24) and engages in very successful agricultural ventures (v.16). And everyone praises her for her significant role in her home, in the community and in the world: her husband (v. 28), her children (v. 28), and her community (v. 31).[71]

The actions of this woman were tremendous, yet she did not undermine her husband. Clearly, she worked within the scope of her role and helped him in successfully doing the work of God in fulfillment of God's word.

Miriam is another woman of Old Testament significance. She was a prophetess (Exod. 15:20) who was directly involved in the early years of her younger brother, Moses (Exod. 2:4-8). Miriam led the Hebrew women in a celebration of praise following the nation's deliverance from Egypt (Exod. 15:20-21). The prophet Micah presented Miriam in a favorable light by naming her with Moses and Aaron as leaders (Mic. 6:4). However, Miriam, along with Aaron, challenged Moses' authority in Numbers 12.[72] Charles Ready Nichol (1876–1961), a legendary preacher and author among the Churches of Christ, describes Miriam's actions in this text:

> Have you noticed that when the name Miriam appears in connection with that of Moses and Aaron's, her name appears last, with the one exception found in Numbers twelfth chapter and first verse? In this verse it reads, "Miriam and Aaron." It is my view that her name appears first in this passage because it is detailing the rebellion, in which Miriam was the leader, the revolt originated with her. This case furnishes an example of what it means for a woman to usurp authority over a man.[73]

The Lord's response was severe: He struck Miriam with leprosy (Num. 12:20). In this case, her actions adversely affected the nation because they did not journey for seven days while Miriam was outside of the camp (Nm 12:14-15).

Deborah, a prophetess, is another remarkable woman from the Old Testament (Judg. 4:4). Julia P. Craig-Horne named Deborah as one of the common arguments for women clergy.[74] However, Barbara K. Mouser, a self-proclaimed homemaker, author, and speaker, presented a compelling argument for the complementarian view. Mouser described the seven principles of Deborah based on the text of Judges 4 and 5. These principles include: the womanliness of Deborah; Deborah is not a judge in the sense of being a military deliverer; Deborah accommodates and cooperates with

Barak; Deborah is a wife and mother; Deborah does not lead or fight in the battle; Deborah arises as a mother rather than a judge or warrior; and Deborah is commanded to sing and not take captives.[75] Furthermore, Mouser made an even stronger assertion in the following:

> Women taking men's roles is [sic] an abnormality, not a freedom. Women were never anointed to be kings, priests, warrior judges, apostles, or elders. On rare occasions they were prophetesses. There is no precedent in Deborah for matriarchy or women's ordination. To use the rare and exceptional woman as a fulcrum for overturning the gender standards of Scripture and nature is as pervasive today as it is aberrant. Because a woman is gifted, smart, competent, or visionary is not an excuse for giving her the offices and duties of a man. To do so is a final judgment on men and a displacement of the woman that will prevent her from deploying her strengths in their natural and most effective framework. By her words, Deborah considered it more desirable to arise as a mother than as a judge or even as a prophetess. It is a curse on a people when women and children rule over them, not because women and children are inherently evil, but because it represents a breakdown of God's created order whereby men lead and protect, while women help and nurture for the glory of God and the benefit of all.[76]

The Old Testament reveals the continuation of the created roles of men and women. The Old Testament is focused on the family rather than the individual. The Old Testament is primarily patriarchal. The Old Testament presents a high view of women and there are many admirable and significant women. However, there is no significant evidence that the pattern of creation changed in the Old Testament. Men continued to be head and the women continued as helpers in the word and work of God.

The Role of Men and Women in the Ministry of Jesus Christ

The Inspired Gospel writers, Matthew, Mark, Luke, and John, recorded the earthly life and ministry of Jesus Christ. Since Jesus is the head of the church, His followers should submit to His teaching regarding the role of men and women (Eph. 1:22). Unfortunately, the egalitarian and complementarian followers disagree about the teachings of Jesus Christ on this subject. Both claim to find support for their position in the Gospels.[77] A review of the literature reveals Jesus appealed to the creation narrative concerning matters between men and women, Jesus held a high view of both women and men, and Jesus acknowledged role distinctions between men and women.

When the Pharisees tested Jesus concerning the lawfulness of divorcing a wife, Jesus responded by appealing to the creation narrative of Genesis 1 and 2 (Matt. 19:1-10). Alexander Strauch commented as follows:

> When Jesus was questioned by a delegation of Pharisees about the long-debated issue of divorce, He directed His critics to Genesis 1 and 2. In fact, He quoted Genesis 1:27 and 2:24 as the authoritative source of truth. ... When, responding to the Pharisees' male-centered divorce practice, Jesus declared, "from the beginning it was not so" (Matt. 19:8 NKJV). The Pharisees had failed to understand God's original intention for marriage and the

sexes. Hence Jesus told them to go back to the "beginning," back to the Genesis account of creation, back to the Word of God where they would discover God's normative design for marriage. The same is true for us today. If we want to understand God's will for the sexes, we must follow Christ's example. When Jesus and His chief representatives, Peter and Paul, wanted to recapture the original design for marriage and gender, they used Genesis, the book of "beginnings."[78]

Clearly, the role of the husband is not to divorce his wife and the role of the wife is not to divorce her husband (Mark 10:11-12). Although the text does not specifically discuss the roles of men and women, it does validate the importance of the creation account in understanding the role relationship between men and women.[79] Strauch drew several interesting conclusions about roles based on Genesis 2: God made Adam the central character, God created Adam first, God formed the woman out of the man, God created the woman for the man, God gave the man the right to name the woman, and God created the man and women equal in nature.[80]

Each of the Gospel writers revealed that Jesus held a high view of both women and men. James A. Borland, (Professor, New Testament and Theology, Liberty Baptist Theological Seminary) wrote:

Jesus' high regard for women is seen in how He recognized their intrinsic equality with men, in how He ministered to women, and in the dignity He accorded to women during his ministry. Jesus' recognition of role distinctions for men and women is demonstrated by His choosing only men to serve as His apostles with their primary tasks of preaching, teaching, and governing. Women, however, served in other important capacities, such as praying, providing financial assistance, ministering to physical needs, voicing their theological understanding, and witnessing to the resurrection.[81]

Jesus treated all people, including women, with love and respect as He presented the truth. His compassion and wisdom are unmatched. There are numerous examples and ample evidence of the Lord's ceaseless care for people regardless of gender in the four Gospels.[82]

Larry Chouinard, (Professor, New Testament, Kentucky Christian College) summarized the Lord's view and interaction with women in the Gospel of Matthew:

In Matthew's story, neither gender nor social status are categories that explicitly define discipleship or ministerial participation. Readers of this Gospel are led to evaluate female characters in a positive way because of their faith and acts of service, not because they are aligned with contemporary standards or limitations associated with gender. It appears that this emphasis on the paradigmatic function of women as exemplary of Christian discipleship and service is reflective also of the early churches' struggle to work out the kingship of God in a world divided according to socio-economic, racial, and sexual distinctions.[83]

Frederick D. Aquino and A. Brian McLemore, both Master of Divinity graduates from Abilene Christian University, described the Lord's high view of women in the Gospel of Mark:

Women, like other characters, develop the plot of Mark's story and reveal his kingdom point of view. Women are not devalued (e.g. Munro), neither do they represent true, ideal, or perfect disciples (e.g. Fiorenza), but they illustrate certain characteristics of discipleship, essential for Jesus' followers in any age (e.g. Malbon). In God's domain, neither status, wealth, gender, purity, or race determine one's position. What one does, not who one is, initiates one into the kingdom of God. Mark wrote his story for a community; but his message about the kingdom is not captive to any one situation. Neither can any contemporary theology, whether fundamentalist or feminist, impose its agenda on Mark's story or character. Mark's narrative calls all to accept God's vision and resist the temptation to rule his story.[84]

Allen Black (Associate Professor, New Testament, Harding Graduate School of Religion) summarized the Lord's attitude and actions toward women in the Gospel of Luke as follows:

Luke's interest in the fulfillment of the prophecies concerning the restored people of God provides a theological explanation for his inclusion of many women and men-women parallels in Luke-Acts. Through both volumes of his work, Luke demonstrates that men and women are healed, hear Jesus' teaching, become disciples, bear witness, receive the Spirit, prophesy, and receive salvation. For Luke, this is not a matter of being pro- or anti-feminist, or of seeking to relieve women from oppression within a patriarchal framework, but rather a matter of demonstrating how God has kept his promises to Israel and to the nations.[85]

Bonnie Thurston, (former William F. Orr Professor, New Testament, Pittsburgh Theological Seminary) summarized the Lord's high view of women and men in John's Gospel as follows:

> The overall picture of women in John, then, as it is in Mark's Gospel, is very positive. Women are depicted as independent followers of Jesus. Only two women, Mary, the mother of Jesus, and Mary, the wife of Clopas, are introduced in relationship to men. John's women played unconventional roles of which Jesus appears to have approved, sometimes overruling the men who objected ... Women and men were commissioned as agents of the word and stood at the foot of the cross as representatives of Jesus' true family. It is not irresponsible to draw the conclusion that in the community of John the evangelist, women and men must have exhibited a considerable degree of equality in the life of discipleship.[86]

The Lord's high view of women as evidenced by the four Gospels does not negate the fact that He did make role distinctions based on gender. James A. Borland wrote:

> Christ not only valued women very highly, but also demonstrated clear role distinction between men and women. Nowhere is this issue seen more clearly than in Jesus' selection of only men for the role of apostle.[87]

Luke 6:12-16 recorded the selection process of His closest followers. Jesus prayed prior to the selection of apostles. After the Lord called the disciples to Him, He chose twelve of them to be apostles. The Lord did not choose everyone. He chose a limited number of men. Bonnie Thurston, however, described Mary Magdalene as "the apostle to the apostles."[88] This is an unfortunate assertion because the Scripture never refers to her as an apostle. According to James A. Borland, the apostles were more than messengers because Christ trained them firsthand (Mark 3:14-15), they were the leaders in the early church (Acts 2:14; 5:12, 18, 40, 42; 6:2-4; 9:29; 15:2; Gal. 1:17), they received special rulership (Matt. 19:28; Luke 22:30), they received special revelation (John 16:13-15) and special teaching ministry of the Holy Spirit (John 14:26), and their names are forever inscribed on the twelve foundations (Rev. 21:14).[89]

Borland also wrote:

> None of the above roles was performed by the women who followed Christ or ministered to Him. Though highly valued and given a new dignity by Christ, their roles were different from those of the men Christ selected for His top leadership positions. Women gave to Christ, served Him, fellowshipped with Him, accompanied Him, learned from Him, prayed, and testified of their salvation or of Christ's resurrection. But no woman in Christ's ministry was called, commissioned, or named as an apostle, or even performed in the role of an apostle. These roles and functions Christ reserved for men.[90]

The life and ministry of Jesus Christ as recorded in the Gospels does not negate the value and importance of both women and men.

It does, however, present ample evidence Jesus Christ validated the importance of the creation account, highly valued women, and made role distinctions between men and women. Both egalitarians and complementarians attempt to justify their positions by the Gospels.

The Role of Husbands and Wives in the New Testament

God created husbands and wives to share in a mutually satisfactory God-directed covenant relationship. The husband and wife become one in marriage (Gen. 2:24). God created a form of leadership for the marriage covenant. Everett Ferguson, a distinguished scholar, attested to the importance of leadership within the husband-and-wife relationship:

> Any social group has to have some form of leadership. This applies to the smallest and most basic unit of human society, the family. In the family, this leadership is assigned to the husband/father. Not every male, just because of reaching an age of accountability, is given authority in a family (see Luke 2:42, 51)–the same is true for the church.[91]

Furthermore, the Scriptures bear witness to the need for and importance of leadership. God selected Moses to be a leader in the campaign to liberate Israel from Egypt (Exod. 3:10). Following the wise counsel of Jethro, Moses taught and selected other leaders to assist in serving the people (Exod. 18:13-27). God appointed Joshua as leader after the death of Moses (Josh. 1:1-9). Robert D. Dale also attested to the presence of leaders in the Scriptures when he wrote:

The Bible is filled with rich models for pastoral leaders. Kings, priests, prophets and prophetesses, sages, Sanhedrin members, family and household authorities, the synagogue structure, the Pharisee and Essene communities, Greek democracy, the secular trade guilds, Roman rulers, pastors and elders, bishops, deacons, apostles, and missionaries provide possibilities for leadership perspectives.[92]

Other experts in the fields of ministry and social psychology describe the importance of leadership. Michael Z. Hackman of the University of Colorado and Craig E. Johnson of George Fox University, both Professors of Communication, asserted leadership is at the core of human experience:

Leadership is all around us. ... Leadership is an integral part of human life in rural tribal cultures as well as in modern industrialized nations. ... Followers prosper under effective leaders and suffer under ineffective leaders whatever the context: government, corporation, church or synagogue, school, athletic team, or class project group.[93]

Additionally, Edwin H. Friedman (1932–1996) underscored the importance of leadership as it relates to the family as follows:

The key to successful spiritual leadership, therefore, with success understood not only as moving people toward a goal, but also in terms of the survival of the family (and its leader), has more to do with the leaders' capacity for self-definition than with the ability to motivate others.[94]

Finally, Gilbert W. Fairholm, (visiting Professor, Political Science, Hampden-Sydney College) described the soul of leadership when he wrote:

> Leaders must get in touch with their own spiritual nature. They must sense the spiritual essence of their followers and must deal directly with the task of creating an organization – defined as a group of people in voluntary relationship – where the essential spiritual needs of each member is considered and made a part of the group experience.[95]

This "soul of leadership" is clearly in view in the context of marriage. The New Testament reveals a sincere concern about the spiritual needs of both husbands and wives. Fairholm's assessment of the "voluntary relationship" is also appropriate in the context of marriage today. The husband and wife choose to enter into this relationship with one another and live under God's direction.

Husbands and wives experience relationships with each other. Friedman described the family as a system.[96] A. Duane Litfin, an assistant professor of Practical Theology, described family in biological terms:

> The traditional understanding of biblical roles in marriage is essentially this: the husband and wife function together in a "symbiotic" relationship. The word symbiosis is a biological term referring to two different organisms living in close association or union, especially where such an arrangement is advantageous to both. The opposite of symbiosis is parasitism, which refers to a relationship in which one organism lives off another organism and derives sustenance and protection

from it without making compensation. God never intended that marriage partners should be leeches on one another; rather, He intended that they should live together in the closest possible harmony, fulfilling complementary and mutually edifying roles, so that both partners might conjointly grow and mature into their full potential. Traditionally, the essence of these complementary, symbiotic roles has been defined in terms of the wife's submission to the authority of her husband, and the husband's selfless care for the needs of his wife.[97]

Various New Testament passages describe this "symbiotic relationship" between the husband and wife (Eph. 5:22-33; Col. 3:18-19; Titus 2:4-5; 1 Pet. 3:1-7). These passages also define the roles of husbands and wives. The definition is inspired and not arbitrary. Christ is the governing source of the roles. The roles are interdependent. Creation rather than culture is the foundation of the roles. The roles do not imply the inferiority or superiority of either husbands or wives.

The Role of the Wife

Through Scripture, the Lord instructs the wife to submit to her husband (Eph. 5:22; Col. 3:18; 1 Pet. 3:1). The disagreement between egalitarians and complementarians is not what the Scripture says, but what it means. Egalitarians reject the idea of female submission in part because of abuse and discrimination.[98] Wayne Grudem, (Associate Professor, Biblical and Systematic Theology) acknowledged the importance of clarifying what submission does not mean while discussing 1 Peter 3:1-7. These assertions are even more meaningful because Grudem is a complementarian. Grudem asserted that: 1) submission does not mean putting a husband in the place of Christ; 2) submission does not mean giving up independent thought; 3) submission does not mean a wife should give up efforts to influence and guide her husband; 4) submission does not mean a wife should give in to every demand of her husband; 5) submission is not based on lesser intelligence or competence; 6) submission does not mean being fearful or timid; and 7) submission is not inconsistent with equality in Christ.[99]

The wife's submission is not derogatory or forced.[100] A husband does not have the right to force his wife into submission.[101] Submission is a voluntary surrender of personal rights.[102] Submission expresses the attitude of placing oneself at the disposal of another.[103] Submission is a willful deference.[104] Kenneth V. Neller, (Assistant Professor, New Testament, Harding University) described the wifely submission" of Ephesians 5 as follows:

> In the same way that the church voluntarily submits itself to Christ (5:24), a wife voluntarily submits herself to her husband. She is not subjugated unwillingly. A Christian husband no more subjugates his wife to his will through intimidation or force than Christ forcibly subjugates the church to his will. Christ subjugates his enemies, but not his disciples. By placing wifely submission in the context of Jesus and his church, Paul clearly teaches that the husband-wife relationship should not be one of animosity, antagonism, servitude, or oppression, but one of love and respect.[105]

The submission of the wife in the New Testament connects with the role of helper established at creation in Genesis 2:18-25.

The Role of the Husband

The husband's corresponding role is "head of the wife."[106] Alexander Strauch defined head as follows:

> The word *head (kephale)* is used in the figurative sense of "one in authority over," or "leader." When Scripture says, "the husband is the head of the wife," it means he is the leader of the two people, the authority figure. The word "head" *does not* mean "source of" or "origin."[107]

Headship, however, is not demanding, bossy, or overbearing. George W. Knight III explained this as follows:

> Paul also addresses the danger of husbands' being overbearing toward their wives, or "harsh with them" (Colossians 3:19). Paul alludes to that attitude in Ephesians in his remark that "no one ever hated his own body" (Ephesians 5:29), and in the Colossians account (where he does not develop the concept of love as he does in Ephesians) he explicitly demands as a corollary to the command, "Husbands, love your wives," the parallel command, "do not be harsh with them."[108]

The headship taught in the New Testament is rooted in love. Again, Knight explained:

> In so doing Paul emphasizes that the headship of the husband over his wife must not be negative, oppressive, or reactionary. Instead, it must be a headship of love in which the husband gives

himself for his wife's good, nourishing and cher-
ishing the beloved one who, as his equal, volun-
tarily submits to his headship. Paul has thus given
two great truths with respect to the husband: first,
that he is the head of his wife, and second, that he
must exercise his headship in love.[109]

Furthermore, the husband's headship demands loving protection. Strauch wrote:

Likewise, Christian husbands are, in the highest
sense, to love their wives. They are to give their
all for their wives — even their lives if necessary
(v. 25). They are to protect their wives from evil
influences and cultivate their spiritual perfection
and beauty.[110]

The New Testament instructs husbands to provide ser-
vant-based leadership toward their wives and families. The husband's function derives from his position.[111] Neller described the
role of husbands as servants as follows:

Like Christ, husbands are to become servants (Phil.
2:5-7; Mark 10:45), be patient, kind, and compas-
sionate (Matt. 11:19; Rom. 5:6-8), lead by example
(John 13:15; 1 John 3:16), love their wives as their
own bodies (Eph. 5:28, 33), nurture and care for
their wives (Eph. 5:29-31) and give their lives
(Eph. 5:25; Acts 20:28; Tit. 2:14; Mark 8:34-35).[112]

The husband's servant leadership includes providing spiritual nourishment and loving care (Eph. 5:29), giving her intimate affection (1 Cor. 7:4), praying with her and for her (1 Cor.

7:5), and treating her with consideration and respect (1 Pet. 3:7). Furthermore, the husband's servant leadership demands provision for his wife (1 Tim. 5:8).

Husbands would do well to strive for the qualities described in 1 Timothy 3:1-13.[113] These spiritual qualities must be manifest in husbands and fathers before they may become overseers and deacons in the church. In other words, the demonstration of successful servant leadership in the family is a prerequisite to servant leadership in the church.

Men and Women in the New Testament Family and Church

The New Testament deploys the language of family to describe the Church. Vern Sheridan Poythress, (Professor, New Testament Interpretation, Westminster Theological Seminary) highlighted several New Testament texts that demonstrate this analogy: God is Father (Matt. 6:9); the redeemed are children of God (Gal. 4:1-7); saints have an intimate family fellowship with God (Rom. 8:14-17); saints have the privilege of reflecting the Father's holy character (1 Pet. 1:14-17); and only Christians can cry "Abba, Father" (Rom. 8:15).[114]

There is a close relationship between the organizational design of the family and the church. Everett Ferguson wrote:

> The church in its organization reflects God's plan for the family. In fact, the church is described as a family. The Greek word *oikos* may refer to a house, a dwelling place, a building; and in this sense on occasion refers to the dwelling place, a building; and in this sense on occasion refers to the dwelling place of deity, a temple. The word also may refer to those who dwell in a house, the household, or family.[115]

Vern Sheridan Poythress agreed with Ferguson. He was convinced that 1 Timothy referenced those in the church family. He wrote:

> But in the context of 1 Timothy, the idea of household order and arrangements is obviously the most prominent. The order of the church is analogous to the order of a human household. Members of the church are to treat one another as they would members of their own family (1 Timothy 5:1-2). They are to care for one another in need (1 Timothy 5:5, 16). The overseers are to be men skillful at managing the household of God, as demonstrated by their earlier skill with their own immediate families (1 Timothy 3:1-7).[116]

In fact, a failure to acknowledge the similarities and connections shared by the family and the church has contributed to the confusion between the roles of men and women. Alexander Strauch described this scenario as follows:

> Many people don't understand the New Testament's view of men and women in the church because they don't understand the intimate relationship between the individual family and the extended family, which is the local church. Just as Paul teaches masculine leadership in the individual family, he teaches masculine leadership in the extended local church family. So an understanding of leadership in the family is essential to an understanding of leadership in the church family.[117]

In this work, we seek to increase the understanding of this relationship among the men and women within the body of Christ. An important understanding is the model of male leadership in both the family and the church. Everett Ferguson described this idea:

> Leadership in the church corresponds to leadership in the family. As indicated above, the leadership in the family derives from the pattern set by Christ and the Church. Since the church is a family, we should expect the same principles of organization to be operative in the church as apply to the family, and indeed this is true. Leadership in the church is given to male family heads, not to all males.[118]

Therefore, deficiencies in family leadership such as single-parent homes, divorce, spiritually mixed marriages, and abandonment of responsibility will adversely affect the church. Alexander Strauch explained it as follows:

It is becoming increasingly difficult to find biblically qualified and prepared men to assume the responsibilities of church eldership and deaconship. The hyper-busyness of our culture holds many of our men in a spiritual death grip: The cult of busyness and activism that infects Christians so much today is one of the greatest barriers to the church becoming what it should be. Too many men have no time for Bible reading, prayer, or church family leadership. Some don't even have time for their families. When men neglect their community leadership responsibilities within the church community, a tragic loss and a stunning victory for the evil one occurs.[119]

Evangelists

Evangelists are included in God's family.[120] Paul referred to Timothy, an evangelist, as "his son in the faith" (1 Tim. 1:2). Timothy is also included in the house or household of God (1 Tim. 3:15). Evangelists serve God's people within the family (1 Tim. 5:1-2). Harold R. Redd, an African-American evangelist among the Churches of Christ, cautioned Christian ministers to remember their charge as God's servants to serve and sacrifice for His people.[121]

Evangelists are leaders in the local church. However, a debate surrounds the role of the evangelist within the Churches of Christ. Everett Ferguson excluded the evangelist from a leadership role within the church.[122] Harold R. Redd explained the history of the debate:

> White churches generally believed the elders of the church exercised primary authority in the churches. African-American churches were generally led by the parson or the evangelist. J. S. Winston, at the fiftieth Annual National Lectureship of African-American Churches of Christ, talked about the history of that leadership issue. In summary, he explained how white elders often ordained elders in African-American churches to help oversee or watch the preacher, who was in many cases the preacher for the black church and the custodian for the white church. These elder ordinations and the whole approach to appointing elders was strongly resented by African-American ministers in the Churches of Christ. Many preached sermons against elders' rights to ordain elders and about the biblical authority of the evangelist because of this

issue. When elders in African-American churches perceived themselves as having authority over the evangelist, power struggles resulted, and many black preachers became hesitant to ordain elders. Fortunately, this hesitancy is changing as more African-American ministers learn that one gains power by losing it and are more willing to risk control for the development that results when people are trained and empowered.[123]

The evangelist often serves as the primary leader. Redd wrote:

Many African-American Churches of Christ, even ones with elders and deacons, have functioned with a man at the top. This arrangement would not have presented a problem for African culture, but has conflicted with European-American concepts of leadership.[124]

Regardless of one's view, God ordained the role of evangelists.[125] Especially in African-American churches, the evangelist has played a crucial role [126] and has a role outside of the pulpit.[127] In our own experiences as evangelists, the congregation often looks to us for vision and guidance concerning the direction of the church.[128]

The work of the evangelists attests to the leadership role that God gave them in order to prepare the members to do spiritual work (Eph. 4:11-12). Luis R. Lugo, an African-American evangelist in the Churches of Christ, placed the work of the evangelist in five categories based on the New Testament Epistles of 1 and 2 Timothy and Titus:

1. Proclaimer: That is, he is to preach, herald, and proclaim the Gospel.

2. Trainer: He is to train the local church.
3. Organizer: He is to "set in order the things that are lacking."
4. Defender: He is to be set for the defense of the Gospel.
5. Discipliner: He is to discipline heretics.[129]

Evangelists and elders work together. The evangelist and elders are working together in the ministry context of both of our local congregations. Evangelists and Elders have a shared vision and set of values to help guide them toward their goals and objectives. Luis R. Lugo attested to the importance of the relationship between the evangelist and elders when he wrote:

> Once elders are ordained, the congregation must realize that elders are not superior to the evangelist. It is precisely here that the evangelist and elders must have a strong working relationship, for there are many weak people in the body, who because of likes and dislikes, will pit the evangelist against the elders and vice versa. If the relationship is not right, the church will suffer .... He does not relinquish his authority because elders have been ordained! Elders die, disqualify themselves, move, get old, and lose interest. Therefore, the training and development of men to serve as elders is an ongoing process.[130]

Clearly, a relationship of trust based on mutual love, care, accountability, and respect is vital to sustaining this important Christian relationship.[131]

Evangelists are men and not women. However, Robert M. Randolph, a member of the Churches of Christ, would like to hear the voices of women from our pulpits.[132] Julia Craig-Horne listed a number of arguments both for and against women clergy.[133]

Since the evangelist is a leader within God's family with the afore-mentioned responsibilities, this excludes women from assuming this role. The principles of male headship are applicable in this area as well.[134]

Elders

The New Testament uses various terms to describe elders (James 5:14) such as overseers (1 Pet. 5:2), shepherds (1 Pet. 5:2), pastors (Eph. 4:11), and bishops (Phillippians 1:2).[135] There are several dissertations addressing the role of elders within the Churches of Christ;[136] however, none of them address the roles of men and women.

Elders are men and not women. Alexander Strauch correctly asserted that a Biblical eldership is exclusively male.[137] However, in many denominations women have been ordained in this office.[138] There are significant indications from the New Testament that only men meet the requirements for this important office. One of the qualifications for being an elder is being "the husband of one wife" (1 Tim. 3:2; Titus 1:6). Furthermore, elders must demonstrate their ability to lead their families (1 Tim. 3:4). Luis R. Lugo made this important observation when he wrote:

> Within the home, the man who would be an Elder receives on the job training in anticipation of becoming an elder in the house of the Lord. Let us never forget that the church is the Lord's house and that the men who are going to serve as its leaders must have their own houses in order! This qualification calls for both men of unique faith as well as women of the same quality. The home life of the Elder becomes a picture as to how he will oversee the heritage of God. In this qualification of

117

the home we come into contact with the concepts of fairness, discipline, respect, openness, understanding, problem solving and spiritual development. If one wants to know whether a man has the ability to run the church, just go visit the man's house and observe how his family interacts and respects him. See if he is a tyrant or a bully to his wife and children. Do they submit to his headship? Do they follow his lead and do they manifest a godly attitude towards the spiritual direction of his lead?[139]

Elders are leaders with important responsibilities similar to the husband in the family. Everett Ferguson wisely wrote:

As the husband in the family exercises a leadership of love, so in the church its elders acting as stewards of God's household exercise a loving, serving leadership following the example of Jesus (Matt. 20:25-28; John 13:1-17; 1 Pet. 5:2-4). God's ranking of male and female going back to the creation and fall is reflected in males taking the leadership in the assembly and females following this leadership in respectful silence.[140]

Elders care for the spiritual-well-being of the members. According to Lugo,[141] the work of elders includes: watching (Acts 20:28-31), admonishing (2 Thess. 3:6-15), feeding and tending the flock (1 Pet. 5:1-5; Acts 20:28), ruling or guiding (Heb. 13:17, 24; 1 Tim. 5:20), maturing the church (Eph. 4:11), visiting and praying for the sick (James 5:13-18), and overseeing (1 Pet. 5:1).

African-American Churches of Christ are having trouble with elders because they are experiencing difficulties with their families.

Harold R. Redd asserted that ministering to the African-American family will be one of the greatest challenges facing the African-American church in the next century.[142] Redd also expressed concern for the African-American male:

A major concern for the black family is the plight of the black male. Black families must reclaim black males from prison cells and diseased communities that led them there, and the church must take part in that reclamation process.[143]

Others agree there are serious concerns about the African-American family and males in particular. Psychology professors Derald Wing Sue and David Sue asserted some have perhaps, in a dehumanizing manner, categorized the African-American male as an endangered species due to a higher mortality rate than white males.[144] Furthermore, slavery undermined the role of the African-American husband and hindered his ability to provide for his family and protect them.[145] Wilma A. Dunaway, (Associate Professor, Sociology, Virginia Polytechnic Institute and State University) described the structured absence of the slave husband and father.[146] Dunaway asserted that the slave marriage had no legal rights.[147] Additionally, masters often broke up slave families through sales. Wilma Dunaway wrote:

When Thomas Jefferson died, the families of 130 slaves were permanently separated. The five days of auctioning were so traumatic that it reminded one of Jefferson's grandchildren of "a captured village in ancient times when all were sold as slaves."[148]

Several factors contributed to the disempowerment of the African-American slave husband and father. In many cases, the husband and father did not live with the wife and children.[149] The slave master restricted the male slave's contact with his family, often only allowing a weekend visit.[150] The children lived with the mother in her house.[151] The slave father did not usually discipline the slave children.[152] The slave children were considered the property of the mother's master,[153] as indicated by wearing the master's surname.[154]

The plight of the African-American context has struck a blow against the family. In many cases, the African-American male is disadvantaged in comparison to the African-American female. In one of the many illustrative articles in *The Covenant*,[155] David M. Satcher, Interim President of the Morehouse School of Medicine and former Surgeon General of the United States, wrote:

> There are also gender differences among African Americans that relate to income gains experienced by African-American women and the provision of Medicaid, which is more amenable to black women than to black men. Violence and gun-related deaths have taken a toll on African-American men. Disproportionate numbers of black men are incarcerated as a result of policies that mandate imprisonment as opposed to treatment for substance abuse.[156]

Furthermore, Paulette Moore Hines and Nancy Boyd-Franklin described this disparity concerning gender roles and couple relationships among African-Americans as follows:

> African-American women, who are often more actively religious than their mates, are frequently

regarded as the "strength of the family." More easily employed than their male counterparts, Black women historically have worked outside the home, sometimes as the sole wage earners, particularly in times of high unemployment.[157]

The church cannot have elders without having African-American men that are leading their families with godly headship. Slavery has influenced the African-American experience. Slavery adversely affected the family. William Lynch, a white slave owner in the 1700s, described his psychological methods of "breaking slaves":

Pay little attention to the generation of original breaking but concentrate on future generations. Therefore, if you break the female mother, she will break the offspring in its early years of development and, when the offspring is old enough to work, she will deliver it up to you for her normal female protective tendencies will have been lost in the original breaking process.[158]

Lynch also compared African slaves to horses to be bred and broken:

Take the meanest and most restless nigger, strip him of his clothes in front of the remaining male niggers, the female, and the nigger infant, tar and feather him, tie each leg to a different horse in opposite directions, set him afire and beat both horses to pull him apart in front of the remaining niggers. The next step is to take a bullwhip and beat the remaining nigger male to the point of death in front of the female and infant. Don't kill him, but put the fear of God in him, for he can be useful for future breeding.[159]

Lynch described the process of breaking the African woman:

In this frozen psychological state of independence she will raise her male and female offspring in reversed roles. For fear of the young male's life, she will psychologically train him to be mentally weak and dependent, but physically strong. Because she has become psychologically independent, she will train her female offspring to be psychologically independent. What have you got? You've got the nigger woman out front and the man behind and scared. This is a perfect situation for sound sleep and economics.[160]

Furthermore, Lynch described the assault against the family:

Continually, though the breaking of uncivilized savage niggers, by throwing the nigger female savage into a frozen psychological state of independency, by killing of the protective male image by creating a submissive dependent mind of the nigger male savage, we have created an orbiting cycle that turns in its own axis forever, unless a phenomenon occurs and re-shifts the positions of the female savages.[161]

Lynch's comments on the marriage unit or reproduction process are quite relevant to this issue. He wrote:

We breed two nigger males with two nigger females.
Then we take the nigger males from them and keep
them moving and working. Say the one nigger
female bears a nigger female and the other bears
a nigger male. Both nigger females, being without
the influence of the nigger image, frozen with an
independent psychology, will raise their offspring
into reverse positions. The one with the female offspring will teach her to be like herself, independent
and negotiable (we negotiate with her, through her,
and by her and negotiate her at will). The one with
the nigger male offspring, she being frozen with
a subconscious fear for his life, will raise him to
be mentally dependent and weak, but physically
strong—in other words, body over mind. Now in
a few years when these two offspring become fer-
tile for early reproduction, we will make and breed
them and continue the cycle. That is good, sound,
and long range comprehensive planning.[162]

Although greatly improved, the impact of slavery on the
African-American family continues to damage leadership potential.
While serving as a distinguished professor at Harvard University,
Cornell West described the present crisis of black leadership when
he wrote, "Presently, black communities are in shambles, black
families are in decline, and black men and women are in conflict
(and sometimes combat)."[163]

Since many African-American "families are in decline," it
makes it more challenging to develop men to serve as elders. It
takes some congregations several decades before they have a qualified plurality of men desiring to serve as elders in the local church.

Deacons

Deacons are servants in the church.[164] Ferguson asserted that deacons serve under the elders.[165] Strauch believed deacons have authority along with elders,[166] while Lugo claimed deacons serve under both the evangelist and elders.[167] Common areas of responsibility for deacons include: benevolence, finances, education, maintenance, and whatever is necessary for the growth of the church.[168] Although the qualification to be the husband of one wife would exclude women from assuming the official role of deacon, some do argue the point (1 Tim. 3:12). Everett Ferguson called it "an open question" in his writing:

> It is an open question whether women were recognized for their services to the church as female deacons. Romans 16:1-2 says of Phoebe, "I commend to you our sister Phoebe, a servant [*diakonos*, deacon] of the church at Cenchreae, ... for she has been a benefactor of many and of myself as well." A benefactor or patron(ess) was a person with resources who provided for others and received duties from them in return. Since the predominant use of *diakonos* in the New Testament is as general term and only seldom as a technical term for an appointed and representative servant of the church (as in Phil. 1:1 and 1 Tim. 3:8), it may be too much (although possible) to claim the latter meaning for Phoebe. First Timothy 3:11, on the other hand, has a better claim to refer to women deacons, but the meanings "wives" or (less likely) "women servants" cannot be ruled out. The position of deacon (=servant) was a serving role.[169]

Others claim the reality of female deacons in early church history. H. Wayne House wrote:

> The office of deaconess is not certain in the New Testament church, but the preponderance of evidence suggests that women had this ministry, for it is certainly seen in the postapostolic period.[170]

Still others like Alexander Strauch argued against ordaining women to the office of deacon.[171] Strauch asserted that the three common interpretations of 1 Timothy 3:11 are women deacons, deacons' assistants, and wives of deacons.[172] Although Strauch made his argument based on his perceived notion of a deacon's authority , others do agree with the conclusion that the role of deacon is limited to men.[173]

Women

If women cannot serve as evangelists, elders, or deacons, what are their ministerial options? John Jefferson Davis, while assistant professor of Theology at Gordon-Conwell Theological Seminary, captured the nature of the present problem as follows:

> In our own contemporary situation we are likewise faced with increasing confusion about our role identities as men and women. For the past two centuries, the process of industrialization and urbanization has moved the populations of the West from the farms, with their relatively clear and traditional role identities, into the increasingly bureaucratized cities, where traditional identities have become eroded. The recent impact of the feminist movement, the pressure for the equal rights amendment,

and the gay liberation movement have called into question traditional understandings of sexual roles as well as their Biblical and theological foundations. There is much uncertainty, both inside and outside of the Church, about what it means to be a man or a woman in our contemporary situation. The proper roles of men and women in marriage and family, in the Church, and in the wider society are the subject of an ongoing debate that has touched us all.[174]

The inspired writers of the New Testament appealed to creation when it came to the role of women in the church (1 Tim. 2:13-15; 1 Cor. 14:35). Neil R. Lightfoot, a prominent Christian scholar, wrote:

It is interesting that in each case where women are forbidden to speak or teach in church, Paul appeals to the original created order and what the law says. His arguments are based not on custom but on Old Testament Scripture.[175]

When applying the New Testament principles, Lightfoot described the limitations of women in the church:

Women in the assembly are to learn in all submissiveness, and they are not to teach men. Otherwise, how could the woman teach, or preside in the meeting, and still be subject to one of the members in the meeting, her husband?[176]

In response to those claiming female liberation based on Galatians 3:28, Ferguson wrote:

Just as a person in Christ continues to be a Jew
or a Gentile, slave or free, so one does not cease
being male or female. Unlike slavery, a changeable
human institution, but like being born a Jew or a
Gentile, a person's gender is not subject to change
(not naturally—that one can undergo a sex change
operation does not affect the argument here anymore than does a Gentile becoming circumcised or
a Jew having an operation to remove his circumcision). The normal biological, psychological, and
sociological differences between male and female
remain, and so do the regulations pertaining to their
different roles (Eph. 5:22-33).[177]

Christian women in the New Testament were able to make
significant contributions while being restricted from certain roles.
Ferguson asserts that in the New Testament women prophesied
(Acts 2:17-18; 21:9; 1 Cor. 11:5); taught (Acts 18:26; Titus 2:3-5);
helped to advance the Gospel (Phil. 4:3; Rom. 16:7); performed
unspecified work (Rom. 6:6, 12); performed hospitality and served
as benefactors (Acts 16:15, 40; Rom. 16:2); and certain qualified
widows served the church (1 Tim. 5:3-16).[178]

There are many ministry opportunities for women.[179] However,
Luis R. Lugo lamented the failure of African-American Churches
of Christ to utilize women in the work of the church. Lugo wrote:

Black women today are educated, trained, and
capable of doing things within the church that do
not abuse nor disqualify men from their role in
the church. Women are part of the body of Christ
and should not be treated as second-class members simply because there is a prohibition as to
her place in teaching and authority over men in

a public arena. Women today are aggressive and passionate about their contributions in the spiritual arena. The Lord's church must not miss this opportunity to utilize this resource. Women need to know that there is a place of ministry for them in the church. That their talents and abilities will be utilized in areas that bring about fulfillment and joy in ministries.[180]

Ann L. Bowman, while an assistant professor of Biblical Studies at the International School of Theology, proposed a number of ministry opportunities for women based on their spiritual gifts. Bowman includes as opportunities for women to take various teaching roles such activities as Sunday school, vacation Bible school, children's church, neighborhood Bible studies, youth director, director of Christian education, director of women's ministries, curriculum development, writing, and workplace Bible studies. Other opportunities, according to Bowman, include visitation programs, retirement home ministries, telephone outreach surveys, conference speaking, counseling, administrative assistant, choirs, Meals on Wheels, fellowship dinners, church bus driver, pastoral support staff, home Bible studies, ministry to the sick and physically challenged, prayer, website design, creating banners, reporting to the local newspaper, and floral arrangements.[181]

Conclusion

God created humanity in His image and men and women are equal in personal worth and value. God assigned complementary roles to men and women: men are to lead women in fulfilling the work of God and keeping the word of God and women are to help men in this assignment. God's assigned roles for men and women in family, church, and society have not changed. However, how do men and women feel about their assigned roles? Do men and women possess adequate knowledge of their roles in the family, church, and society? Do men feel qualified to lead women in the work and word of God? Are women reluctant to trust men as leaders? Do women feel a lack of appreciation for their contributions in the family, church, and society? Do men possess the training to lead in the family, church, and society?

Discussion Questions

1. How does Creation inform your understanding of the role of men and women?
2. What is the role of the husband?
3. What is the role of the wife?
4. How does the state of the family impact the church?
5. What are some scriptural ways women can serve in the church?

Chapter 15
WAYS TO CELEBRATE MASCULINITY

Providers

God, in His infinite wisdom, made the man bigger, stronger, and more muscular than the woman in order to work and ensure that his family needs were met. The original intent for man was to provide. The original intent for the woman was to procreate. Lest we see the physical evidence. This explains the physical anatomy and the physiological differences between the male and the female. A real man defines himself by providing. Men take pride in what they provide for their families. In our discussions with other men, we often boast about the provisions we have afforded to our families.

Protectors

Our roles as protectors accent why we are bigger, stronger, and have more muscle mass than women. It is the nature of the man to provide and protect his family. It is the nature of the man to solve the family problems. This why when a woman speaks to her husband, he tries to solve and fix the problem. At three o'clock in the morning, when there is a strange noise in the house, the man, the protector, does not send his wife to investigate. When the man, the protector, checks into a hotel room, he sleeps on the side of the bed which is closest to the door. The man, the protector, will hold his wife's hand, lock arm in arm, and puts himself on the side from where the traffic is coming from as they cross a busy street. Being a protector is an innate quality of the man.

Priests

The man is the head of the house as Christ is the head of the church. As we learn in Ephesians 5, a man ought to lead the family in Bible study, in prayer, and to worship, including Sunday school. He must take full responsibility for his families' actions and their attitudes. In other words, the man is responsible even when it's not his fault. *"As for me and my house, we will serve the Lord."* (Josh. 24:15)

All men need a vision, "without vision, the people perish." All men have a vice. All men have a victory.

The inception of Adam's sin set in motion a number of tragic consequences. It changed Adam's ontological paradigm. Man began to see himself from a different and distorted perspective. Man allowed the pervasive knowledge of evil entrance into his cognition and conscience. After disobeying God, Adam saw his own nakedness. He was a witness to his own vulnerability. This knowledge of evil exposed man to his own weakness.

It is reminiscent of James. The bondservant of God and of the Lord Jesus Christ said, "But be doers of the word and not hearers only, deceiving yourselves. For if anyone is a hearer of the word and not a doer, he is like a man observing his natural face in a mirror; for he observes himself, goes away, and immediately forgets what kind of man he was." (James 1:22-24)

Adam heard God's word in the Garden, but he was not a doer of the word. He forgot what kind of man he was! Disobedience and sin destroyed his proper sense of image and identity. Don't forget the kind and quality of man God created!

The Lord created men of value, valor, and vigor!
He created men of character, compassion, and courage!
God created men of substance, spirit, and strength!

The Lord we know, love, and serve created men of...
Promise, provision, and protection!
Love, loyalty, and long-suffering!
Holiness, hope, and heart!
Faith, fatherhood, and forgiveness!
Distinction, determination, and deliverance!

Some men have lost their sense of male and masculine image. Like the man traveling the dangerous road between Jerusalem and Jericho, they have fallen among thieves who stripped them of their clothes. They wounded him. In Proverbs 18:14, we read: **"The spirit of a man will sustain him in sickness, but who can bear a broken spirit."** They departed and left him half-dead.

This is the picture of modern times. Men are only half the men they used to be and many desire to be. They have been robbed and wounded by a feminized society that discounts, diminishes, and demeans their manhood. They have been robbed by historical slavery and segregation. They have been disenfranchised, displaced, and disinherited by broken homes. Many are suffering the curse of fatherlessness.

This is not to suggest that as men we have not contributed to our problems or imply that we are innocent in our current condition. We have made tragic mistakes. We have committed grievous sins. We have perpetuated sick family cycles. However, this affirms that it is important for us to understand the socioeconomic, political, historical, judicial, philosophical, and spiritual context of this challenge. Anyone who denies the impact of poverty, unwed parents, crime, drugs, racism, and fundamental changes in worldviews is ill-prepared to help contribute solutions to the problems and challenges faced by today's man.

There must be a restoration of the biblical image of a man. In the macrocosm of social depravation, we as a society have lost a true sense of manhood. The feminists and those sensitive to the feminist agenda preach a false gospel of egalitarianism. They assert that there is no fundamental difference between men and women and the roles they assume in family, church, and society.

In many ways, men are becoming irrelevant. Dr. King said, "The ultimate measure of a man is not where he stands in moments of comfort, but where he stands at times of challenge and controversy." This is a time of challenge and controversy. What is the biblical image of a man?

We must abandon distorted images of manhood. "At the heart of mature masculinity or manhood is a sense of benevolent responsibility to lead, provide for, and protect women and others in ways appropriate to a man's differing relationships."[4]

Manhood is not measured by our ability to have children, our looks, earning potential, physical prowess, reaching a certain age, drinking, voting, body hair, bass in our voice, or driving. Every man must ask this question: "Who am I?"

Weight is measured in pounds.
Speed is measured by miles per hour.
Liquid is measured by gallons.
Houses are measured by square footage.
Gold and diamonds are measured by carats.
Distance is measured by miles.
Time is measure by hours.

---

[4] John Piper, Recovering Biblical Manhood & Womanhood: A Response to Evangelical Feminisms (Wheaton, Illinois: Crossway Books, 2006), 36.

Hard drives are measured by megabytes.
Genius is measured by IQ.

True manhood is measured in virtue! Virtue is doing what is right when doing wrong is much easier! Albert Einstein said, "Try not to become a man of success but a man of value." A true man is secure in himself and recognizes his obligation to God, his family, his church, his community, country, and government.

A true man leads with a servant's heart, filled with love and endued with compassion and concern about the needs and feelings of his fellow man. A true man lives as a living epistle beyond the walls of a church building. A true man does not leave his family and church vulnerable to risks, attacks, and dangers. Protecting them is one of his utmost concerns. His diligence in fulfilling his responsibilities is demonstrated daily as he vigilantly seeks the spiritual, moral, health, educational, social, and economic prosperity of his people.

Who am I? Dr. King said, "We must have the spiritual audacity to assert our somebody-ness. We must no longer allow our physical bondage to enslave our minds. He who feels that he is somebody, even though humiliated by external servitude, achieves a sense of selfhood and dignity that nothing in all the world can take away."

The Image of the Patriarch

Patriarch is a compound word. Pater meaning father is added to archon meaning leader, chief, ruler, or king. The patriarch is the **male leader** of a family, tribe, or clan. Abraham, Isaac, and Jacob are well-known patriarchs.

Patriarch means father led. The patriarch is the male leader of the family. A leader must assume primary responsibility for his position and work to **define his self** and goals, while staying in touch with the rest of the family if he wants them to follow. The family may resist initially, but if the patriarch can stay in touch with the resisters, the family will usually go along.[182]

Men must understand that not all families and family members will follow their leadership without rebellion, challenge, and opposition. "Successful leadership depends not only on the ability to overcome inertial passivity, but it also must be able to avoid being sidetracked by active sabotage. Another paradox facing people at the top is the predictable fact that followers will work to throw them off course precisely when they are functioning at their best." (Friedman p. 223).

God gives vision to the patriarch. The patriarch must impart that God-given vision to the family. Abraham, Isaac, and Jacob were by no means perfect men. Nevertheless, they were men of faith. Patriarchs are concerned with generational blessing and inheritance. Patriarchs want to leave blessings and inheritance for their future generations.

> Proverbs 13:22: "A good man leaves an inheritance to his children's children, but the wealth of the sinner is stored up for the righteous."

> Proverbs 10:22: "The blessing of the Lord makes one rich, and He adds no sorrow with it."

> Proverbs 13:11: "Wealth gained by dishonesty will be diminished, but he who gathers by labor will increase."

> Proverbs 13:7: "There is one who makes himself rich, yet has nothing; and one who makes himself poor, yet has great riches."

Proverbs 10:4: "He who has a slack hand becomes poor, but the hand of the diligent makes rich."

Proverbs 12:11: "He who tills his land will be satisfied with bread, but he who follows frivolity is devoid of understanding."

Proverbs 12:24: "The hand of the diligent will rule, but the lazy man will be put to forced labor."

The Image of the Priest

We realize all saints are included in the priesthood of believers. In addition, the man is an image of the priest that offers sacrifice and talks to God on behalf of his family. We see this priestly image of the man in Job 1:1-5. Job offered burnt offerings to God because it may have been that his sons have sinned and cursed God in their hearts. This theme is repeated in 1 Peter 3:7.

The Image of the Pastor

The original term for pastor is *poimen,* which is a shepherd or one who tends herds or flocks and not merely feeds them. It is the idea of tender care and vigilant superintendence. Some of the great men of the Bible were shepherds or pastors including Abraham, Jacob, Moses, and David.

Men must pastor and shepherd their families. Remember Psalm 23 because it helps us understand the significance of the shepherd image. We must read **Ezekiel 34:1-6**! Pastoring the family is the training ground and prerequisite to shepherding the church. The pastor will go searching for the lost. The pastor will provide for the flock (1 Tim. 5:8).

The Image of the Prophet

The prophet speaks for God to others. It is the image of one that proclaims the divine message to his family! A man is responsible for teaching his family spiritual truth.

Discussion Questions

1. What does it mean for a man to be the priest of his family?
2. What are some ways the church can celebrate biblical masculinity?
3. Why should biblical masculinity be celebrated?
4. Discuss the biblical principle of patriarchy.

NOTES

1 George Barna, The Power of Vision (Ventura: Regal Books, 1984), 24.

2 David F. Wells, God in the Wasteland (Grand Rapids:1994), 145-146.

3 W.E.B. Du Bois, The Souls of Black Folk (Stilwell: Digireads. com Publishing), 7.

4 James H. Cone, Martin & Malcolm (Maryknoll: Orbis Books), 45.

5 Strong's Hebrew/Greek Definitions in PC Study Bible.

6 John MacArthur, *Acts*. (Chicago: Moody Press, 1994, c1996)

7 Gerhard Kittel, Friedrich Gerhard and G.W Bromiley, (Grand Rapids: W.B. Eerdmans, 1995, c1985). Theological Dictionary of the New Testament.

8 Frank Pittman, Man Enough (New York: The Berkley Publishing Group), introduction.

9 Allen P. Ross, Creation and Blessing (Grand Rapids: Baker Books, 1996), 331.

10 Ibid., p.331.

11 Tom Constable, *Tom Constable's Expository Notes on the Bible, Gen. 17:1* (Galaxie Software, 2003).

12 Ross, 333.

13 Frank Pittman, Grow Up! (New York: St. Martin's Press, 1998), 183.

14 Bruce A. Ware, "Male and Female Complementarity and the Image of God," Journal for Biblical Manhood and Womanhood 7 (2002): 15.

15 Allen P. Ross, *Creation & Blessing*, 112.

16 Michael F. Stitzinger, "Genesis 1-3 and the Male/Female Role Relationship," Grace Theological Journal 2 (1981): 28.

17 Bruce A. Ware, "Male and Female Complementarity and the Image of God," 15-24.

18 Ibid., 18.

19 A.W. Tozer, *The Knowledge of the Holy* (San Francisco: Harper Collins Publishers Inc., 1961), 3.

20 Allen P. Ross, *Creation & Blessing*, 112.

21 Ibid., 112.

22 Charles C. Ryrie, Basic Theology (Wheaton: Victor Books, 1995), 3.

23 Kenneth Daughters, "The Trinity and the Christian," Emmaus Journal 14 (2005): 59.

24 Millard Erickson, Christian Theology 2nd Edition, (Grand Rapids: Baker Books, 1999), 362-363.

25 Bruce A. Ware, "Male and Female Complementarity and the Image of God," 19.

26 Betty Friedan, The Feminine Mystique, (New York: W.W. Norton & Company, Inc., 2001), 19.

27 Ibid., 57-532.

28 Wayne Grudem, Systematic Theology (Grand Rapids: Inter-Varsity Press, 1994), 456.

29 Ibid., 459.

30 Ibid., 459.

31 Ibid., 459.

32 Millard Erickson, Christian Theology 2nd Edition (Grand Rapids: Baker Books, 1998), 363.

33 Robert Letham, "The Man-Woman Debate: Theological Comment," Westminster Theological Journal 52 (1990): 70.

34 David Lee Talley, "Gender and Sanctification: From Creation to Transformation A Comparative Look at Genesis 1-3, the Creation and Fall of Man and the Woman, and Ephesians 5, the Sanctification of the Man and the Woman in a Redemptive Marriage Context," Journal for Biblical Manhood and Womanhood 8 (2003): 8.

35 Michael F. Stitzinger, "Genesis 1-3 and the Male/Female Relationship," 31-34. Stitzinger argued for the headship of the man because (1) man was created prior to woman; (2) man's designation as "Adam' represented the entire race; (3) Adam had leadership responsibility prior to the creation of the woman; (4) the exercise of man's authority was immediately demonstrated in naming the animals; (5) the need for a helper demonstrated man's leadership role (6) the man's headship was revealed in naming his wife; (7) the man must leave his father and mother in order to cleave to his wife; (8) The Lord addressed the man and received a response from him in Genesis 3:9, 11.

36 Wayne Grudem, Systematic Theology, 461.

37 Stanley J. Grenz and Denise Muir Kjesbo, Women in the Church: A Biblical Theology of Women in Ministry (Downers Grove: InterVarsity Press, 1995), 164.

38 Ibid., 162-165.

39 James Swanson, Dictionary of Biblical Languages with Semantic Domains: Hebrew (Old Testament*).* Electronic ed., (Oak Harbor: Logos Research Systems, Inc.), 1997_.

40 K.A. Mathews, Genesis 1-11:26. Electronic ed., The New American Commentary 1A (Nashville: Broadman & Holman Publishers, 2001, c1995), Logos Library System.

41 Raymond C. Ortlund, Jr., "Male-Female Equality and Male Headship," in Recovering Biblical Manhood & Womanhood ed. John Piper & Wayne Grudem, (Wheaton: Crossway Books, 1991), 106.

42 Stanley J. Grenz and Denise Muir Kjesbo, Women in the Church: A Biblical Theology of Women in Ministry, 165.

43 Ibid., 166.

44 Ibid., 166.

45 Wayne Grudem, Systematic Theology, 463.

46 Betty Friedan, The Feminine Mystique, 57.

47 Raymond C. Ortlund Jr., "Male-Female Equality and Male Headship," 107.

48 David Lee Talley, "Gender and Sanctification," 9-10.

49 Michael F. Stitzinger, "Genesis 1-3 and the Male/Female Role Relationship," 38.

50 Ibid., 38-39.

51 Wayne Grudem, Systematic Theology, 463.

52 Wayne Grudem, Systematic Theology, 463. Grudem described the effects of the Fall in terms of a distortion of previous roles and not the introduction of new roles.

53 Raymond C. Ortlund Jr., "Male-Female Equality and Male Headship," 109.

54 Alexander Strauch, Men and Women: Equal Yet Different (Littleton: Lewis and Roth Publishers, 1999), 26.

55 John T. Willis, "Women in the Old Testament," in Essays on Women in Earliest Christianity Volume One, ed. Carroll D. Osburn (Eugene: Wipf & Stock Publishers, 1993), 25.

56 In addressing women directly, Willis addresses the role of men indirectly.

57 John T. Willis, "Women in the Old Testament," 25-26.

58 Ibid., 27.

59 Ibid., 28.

60 Joel F. Drinkard, Jr., "An Understanding of Family in the Old Testament: Maybe Not as Different from Us as We Usually Think," Review and Expositor 98 (2001): 499.

61 Ibid., 488.

62 Guenther Haas, "Patriarchy as an Evil That God Tolerated: Analysis and Implications for the Authority of Scripture," Journal of the Evangelical Theological Society 38 (1995): 322.

63 Ibid., 324-325.

64 Alexander Strauch, Men and Women Equal Yet Different, (Littleton: Lewis & Roth Publishers, 1990), 27.

65 Ibid., 27.

66 William E. Hull, "Woman in Her Place: Biblical Perspectives," Review and Expositor 72 (1975): 11.

67 Ibid., 9-10.

68 For a more complete description of Women in the Old Testament, see J.I. Packer, Merrill C. Tenney, William White, Nelson's Illustrated Manners and Customs of the Bible Electronic Ed. (Nashville: Thomas Nelson, 1995), Logos Library System.

69 John T. Willis, "Women in the Old Testament," 34.

70 Julia P. Craig-Horne, "Problems Concerning Women Moving from the Pew to the Pulpit: The Complementary Roles of Women in the Twenty-First Century African-American Church" (D. Min. Dissertation, Amridge University, 2008).

71 John T. Willis, "Women in the Old Testament," 36-37.

72 Pamela J. Scalise, "Women in Ministry: Reclaiming Our Old Testament Heritage," Review and Expositor 83 (1986): 10.

73 Charles Ready Nichol, God's Woman (Clifton: Nichol Publishing Company, 1938), 24.

74 Julia P. Craig-Horne, "Pew to the Pulpit," 15.

75 Barbara K. Mouser, "The Womanliness of Deborah: Complementarian," Journal for Biblical Manhood and Womanhood 11 (2006): 32-33.

76 Ibid., 34.

77 For an egalitarian position, see John Kohlenberger, "Jesus' Treatment of Women," http://www.cbeinternational.org/new/E-Journal/2008/08summer/08summerkohlenberger.html, accessed July 18, 2008. For a complementarian position, see Alexander Strauch, Men and Women: Equal Yet Different.

78 Alexander Strauch, Men and Women: Equal Yet Different, 15-16.

79 For a more detailed discussion of the roles based on Creation, see 15-22.

80 Alexander Strauch, Men and Women: Equal Yet Different, 20-24.

81 James A. Borland, "Women in the Life and Teachings of Jesus," in Recovering Biblical Manhood and Womanhood, ed. John Piper and Wayne Grudem (Wheaton: Crossway Books, 1991), 113.

82 Ibid., 114.

83 Larry Chouinard, "Women in Matthew's Gospel: A Methodological Study," in Essays on Women in Earliest

Christianity Volume One, ed. Carroll D. Osburn (Eugene: Wipf and Stock Publishers, 1993), 444.

84 Frederick D. Aquino & A. Brian McLemore, "Markan Characterization of Women," in Essays on Women in Earliest Christianity Volume One, ed. Carroll D. Osburn (Eugene: Wipf & Stock Publishers, 1993), 424.

85 Allen Black, "Women in the Gospel of Luke," in Essays on Women in Earliest Christianity Volume One, ed. Carroll D. Osburn (Eugene: Wipf & Stock Publishers, 1993), 468.

86 Bonnie Thurston, Women in the New Testament: Questions and Commentary (Eugene: Wipf & Stock Publishers, 1998), 92.

87 James A. Borland, "Women in the Life and Teachings of Jesus," 120.

88 Bonnie Thurston, Women in the New Testament, 90.

89 James A. Borland, "Women in the Life and Teachings of Jesus," 121.

90 Ibid., 121.

91 Everett Ferguson, Women in the Church (Chickasha, OK: Yeomen Press, 2003), 58-59.

92 Robert D. Dale, Pastoral Leadership, (Nashville: Abington Press, 1986), 25.

93 Michael Z. Hackman and Craig E. Johnson, Leadership: A Communication Perspective 4th Edition (Long Grove: Waveland Press, Inc., 2004), 2.

94 Edwin H. Friedman, Generation to Generation, (New York: The Guilford Press, 1985), 221.

95 Gilbert W. Fairholm, Capturing the Heart of Leadership: Spirituality and Community in the New American Workplace (Westport: Praeger, 2000), 1.

96 Edwin H. Friedman, Generation to Generation, 11-49.

97 A. Duane Litfin, "A Biblical View of the Marital Roles: Seeking a Balance," Bibliotheca Sacra 133 (1976): 332.

98 Even complementarians admit the negative impact of misused hierarchal leadership. See Carl B. Hoch Jr., "The Role of Women in the Church: A Survey of Current Approaches," Grace Theological Journal 8.2 (1987): 244.

99 Wayne Grudem, "Wives Like Sarah, and the Husbands Who Honor Them: 1 Peter 3:1-7," in Recovering Biblical Manhood and Womanhood: A Response to Evangelical Feminism, ed. John Piper and Wayne Grudem (Wheaton: Crossway Books, 1991), 194-195.

100 Osborne declares the husband has no right to demand submission from his wife nor misuse it and the wife is an equal partner in marriage. Grant R. Osborne, "Hermeneutics and Women in The Church," Journal of the Evangelical Theological Society 20 (1977): 350.

101 Neller correctly states that the New Testament does not give any human being authority or power to subjugate anyone against their will using *hupotasso*. Kenneth V. Neller, "Submission in EPH. 5:21-33," in Essays on Women in Earliest Christianity, ed. Carroll D. Osburn (Eugene: Wipf & Stock Publishers, 1993), 247.

102 Ibid., 249.

103 Ibid., 249.

104 Ibid., 249.

105 Ibid., 250.

106 Ibid., 251.

107 Alexander Strauch, Men and Women: Equal Yet Different, 57.

108 George W. Knight III, "Husbands and Wives as Analogues of Christ and the Church," in Recovering Biblical Manhood and

Womanhood, ed. John Piper and Wayne Grudem (Wheaton: Crossway Books, 1991), 173.

109 Ibid., 173.

110 Alexander Strauch, Men and Women: Equal Yet Different, 59.

111 Neller remarked that the "headship" of the husband derives not so much from who he is (male), but by what he does (serve). Kenneth V. Neller, "Submission in EPH. 5:21-33," in Essays on Women In Earliest Christianity Volume 1, ed. Carroll D. Osburn, (Eugene: Wipf & Stock Publishers, 1993), 257.

112 Ibid., 257.

113 The researcher acknowledges these qualifications are for elders and deacons. Strauch asserted, "Since an overseer (elder) must manage his family well, all Christian men should follow that model and strive to be good family leaders." Alexander Strauch, Men and Women: Equal Yet Different, 69.

114 Vern Sheridan Poythress, "The Church as Family: Why Male Leadership in the Family Requires Male Leadership in the Church," in Recovering Biblical Manhood and Womanhood, ed. John Piper and Wayne Grudem (Wheaton: Crossway Books, 1991), 233-234.

115 Everett Ferguson, *Women in the Church*, 56.

116 Vern Sheridan Poythress, "The Church as Family," 235-236.

117 Alexander Strauch, Men and Women: Equal Yet Different, 71.

118 Everett Ferguson, Women in the Church, 59.

119 Alexander Strauch, Men and Women: Equal Yet Different, 75.

120 In Churches of Christ, evangelists are also known as preachers and ministers.

121 Harold R. Redd, "Leadership Training for Congregational Transition: A Case Study in an African-American Church" (D. Min. thesis, Abilene Christian University, 2000), 53.

122 Ferguson assigns exclusive leadership to the elders. Everett Ferguson, Women in the Church, 60.

123 Harold R. Redd, "Leadership Training," 14-15.

124 Ibid., 54.

125 Ibid., 50.

126 Ibid., 51.

127 Ibid., 52.

128 Ibid., 52.

129 Luis R. Lugo, The Five Fold Work of the Evangelist: God's Church Administration (Homewood: L&L Publication, 1999), 16-17.

130 Ibid., 89.

131 Ibid., 88. Lugo describes this as a close intimate relationship.

132 Robert M. Randolph, "Why Women Should Be Preaching in Churches of Christ," 205.

133 Julia Craig-Horne, "Pew to the Pulpit," 12-31.

134 Ibid., 27. Craig-Horne stated, "The scriptures provide clear and concise principles of headship in the church, home, and community," when arguing against women clergy.

135 The NIV uses overseers; however, the KJV and NKJV uses Bishops.

136 See Randall Justin Imel, "Shepherding Wandering Sheep: An Examination of Elder's Attitudes Regarding Inactive Christians" (D. Min. Dissertation, Amridge University, 2007); Stephen Johnson, "A Narrative Model For Forming Pastoral Leaders At The Edgemere Church of Christ" (D. Min. Thesis, Abilene Christian University, 2000); Douglass B. Peters, "Selecting Spiritual Leaders: Spiritual Discernment and the Selection of Church Leaders At the North Davis Church of

Christ" (D. Min. Thesis, Abilene Christian University, 2006); Douglas Leon Hall, "A Road Map For The Shepherds At Meadowlark Church of Christ" (D. Min. Thesis, Abilene Christian University, 2005).

137 Alexander Strauch, Biblical Eldership: Restoring The Eldership to Its Rightful Place in The Church (Littleton: Lewis & Roth Publishers, 1997), 17.

138 See Julia P. Craig-Horne, "Pew to the Pulpit," 11.

139 Luis R. Lugo, The Five Fold Work of the Elder (Homewood: L&L Publication, 2006) 79-80.

140 Everett Ferguson, Women in the Church, 60.

141 Luis R. Lugo, The Five Fold Wok of the Evangelist, 46.

142 Harold R. Redd, "Leadership Training," 34.

143 Ibid., 34.

144 Derald Wing Sue and David Sue, Counseling the Culturally Diverse: Theory and Practice 5th Edition (Hoboken: John Wiley & Sons, Inc., 2008), 191.

145 Ibid., 191.

146 Wilma A. Dunaway, The African-American Family in Slavery and Emancipation (New York: Cambridge University Press, 2003), 54.

147 Ibid., 65.

148 Ibid., 59.

149 Ibid., 61.

150 Ibid., 61.

151 Ibid., 64.

152 Ibid., 64.

153 Ibid., 64.

154 Ibid., 65.

155 *The Covenant* addresses the challenges and problems of African-American life and presents practical and responsible actions for African Americans to take. Among the problems and concerns are housing, education, racial profiling, health-care, and injustice.

156 David M. Satcher, "Securing the Right to Healthcare and Well-Being," in The Covenant, ed. Tavis Smiley (Chicago: Third World Press, 2006), 5.

157 Paulette Moore Hines and Nancy Boyd-Franklin, "African American Families," in Ethnicity & Family Therapy 3rd Edition, eds. Monica McGoldrick, Joe Giordano, and Nydia Garcia-Preto (New York: Guilford Press, 2005), 90.

158 Some object to the authenticity of this letter. However, the researcher believes its' popularity speaks to a sense of significance. Even if one doubts the originality of the letter, they cannot deny innumerable abuses, injustices, and murders of African slaves and Negroes in the United States. The Willie Lynch Letter and The Making of a Slave, (Bensenville: Lushena Books, 1999), 14.

159 Ibid., 15.

160 Ibid., 17.

161 Ibid., 17.

162 Ibid., 19.

163 Cornell West, Race Matters (New York: Vintage Books, 1993), 56.

164 The term deacon means servant. Luis R. Lugo, The Five Fold Work of the Evangelist, 56.

165 Everett Ferguson, Women in the Church, 9.

166 Alexander Strauch, "Women Deacons, Deacons Assistants, or Wives of Deacons?," Emmaus Journal 1 (1992): 196-214.

167 Luis R. Lugo, The Five Fold Work of the Evangelist, 57.

168 Ibid., 57.

169 Everett Ferguson, Women in the Church, 9.

170 H. Wayne House, "A Biblical View of Women in the Ministry: Part 4 The Ministry of Women in the Apostolic and Postapostolic Periods," Bibliotheca Sacra 145 (1988): 391.

171 Alexander Strauch, "Women Deacons, Deacons' Assistants, or Wives of Deacons?", 196-214.

172 Ibid., 196-214.

173 Lugo, when describing deacons mentions men only. Luis R. Lugo, The Five Fold Work of the Evangelist, 58.

174 John Jefferson Davis, "Some Reflections on Galatians 3:28, Sexual Roles, and Biblical Hermeneutics," Journal of the Evangelical Theological Society 19 (1976): 202.

175 Neil R. Lightfoot, The Role of Women: The New Testament Perspectives, (Memphis: Mercury Printing, 1978), 37.

176 Ibid., 39.

177 Everett Ferguson, Women in the Church, 67.

178 Everett Ferguson, Women in the Church, 7-9.

179 See Wayne Grudem, "But What Should Women Do in the Church?," Journal for Biblical Manhood and Womanhood 1:2 (November 1995).

180 Luis R. Lugo, "The Church in Transition," The Revivalist (April-June 2008): 18.

181 Ann L. Bowman, "Women, Spiritual Gifts, and Ministry," Faith and Mission 14 (1996): 69-70.

182 Edwin H. Friedman.

CPSIA information can be obtained
at www.ICGtesting.com
Printed in the USA
FFOW05n1817160517

9 781545 604939